MW00986593

To:

_____

From:

_____

Date:

_____

Message:

_____

_____

_____

STORMIE OMARTIAN

A LITTLE BOOK
of
POWERFUL
PRAYERS

HARVEST HOUSE PUBLISHERS

EUGENE, OREGON

Cover by Koechel Peterson & Associates, Inc., Minneapolis, Minnesota

Cover photo © Hemera / Thinkstock

Back cover author photo © Michael Gomez Photography

The prayers in this book are taken from *The Power of Praying® Through the Bible* and *The Power of a Praying® Life*.

A LITTLE BOOK OF POWERFUL PRAYERS
Copyright © 2011 by Stormie Omartian
Published by Harvest House Publishers
Eugene, Oregon 97402
www.harvesthousepublishers.com

ISBN 978-0-7369-2856-4

Printed in China

11 12 13 14 15 16 17 18 19 / RDS-SK / 10 9 8 7 6 5 4 3 2 1

THE BREATH OF LIFE

"The Lord God formed the man from the dust of the ground and breathed into his nostrils the breath of life, and the man became a living being."

GENESIS 2:7

LORD, I thank You for the breath of life You have given me. I pray You will breathe new life into me today. Just as You spoke and brought about life in Your magnificent world, help me to speak words that bring life into my own small world as well. How grateful I am to be closely connected to You in every way. Thank You that You created me for Your purpose.

A Walk in the Garden

"Then the man and his wife heard the sound of the Lord God as he was walking in the garden in the cool of the day, and they hid from the Lord God among the trees of the garden. But the Lord God called to the man, 'Where are you?'"

GENESIS 3:8-9

LORD, I want more than anything to have a close walk with You. Help me to not forfeit that wonderful intimacy by being drawn toward the distractions of this world. Enable me to hear Your voice calling me so that I will answer without even a moment's delay. Help me to never hide from You for any reason. I don't want anything to separate me from all You have for my life.

Powerful Listening

"Noah was a righteous man, blameless among the people of his time, and he walked with God."

Genesis 6:9

Dear God, help me to live each day with a deep sense of Your presence. I don't want to go through life without taking time to be with You. I want my relationship with You to be so strong that other people recognize Your Spirit in me. Whenever I draw near to You in prayer, help me to hear Your voice speaking to my heart so that I will always follow Your leading. Let it be known of me that I walk with You.

THE POWER OF
GOD'S PROMISE

*"Whenever the rainbow appears in the
clouds, I will see it and remember the
everlasting covenant between God and all
living creatures of every kind on the earth."*

GENESIS 9:16

LORD, I thank You that You always keep Your promises to me. Help me to understand and remember exactly what Your promises are so that I can recall them in my mind, keep them in my heart, and speak them out loud whenever I need to push doubt away from me. Help me to remember that Jesus is the ultimate proof that You have already kept Your greatest promise to us. Thank You that He has promised to return.

When We Have to Wait

*"After this, the word of the LORD came
to Abram in a vision: 'Do not be afraid,
Abram. I am your shield, your very great
reward'...Abram believed the LORD, and
he credited it to him as righteousness."*

Genesis 15:1,6

DEAR GOD, help me to have faith enough to
believe You will answer my prayers. Give me the
patience to wait for the answers to appear. Keep
me from giving up and taking matters into my
own hands. Instead, enable me to trust that You
have heard my prayers and will answer in Your perfect way and time. Help me to rest in peace during times of waiting, knowing that my strong faith
pleases You.

MAKING SACRIFICES

*"Some time later God tested Abraham. He
said to him, 'Abraham!' 'Here I am,' he
replied. Then God said, 'Take your son, your
only son, Isaac, whom you love, and go to
the region of Moriah. Sacrifice him there as
a burnt offering on one of the mountains I
will tell you about.' Early the next morning
Abraham got up and saddled his donkey…"*

GENESIS 22:1-3

LORD, I know You want me to surrender everything to You—including the dream in my heart.
And even when that dream is from You, You still ask
me to let go of my hold of it. So I surrender every
dream in my heart to You right now. I don't want to
cling to something You will not bless, or give up on
something that is Your will for my life. I know my
greatest blessing comes in trusting You.

A Prayer for Success

"Then he prayed, 'O Lord, God of my master Abraham, give me success today, and show kindness to my master Abraham.'"

Genesis 24:12

Heavenly Father, I pray for success in all I do. Guide me in everything. Show me where I have proceeded with something without first inquiring of You. Enable me to understand Your measure of success and not try to impose my own. My goal is to serve You, knowing that any success I have will be achieved only by walking perfectly in Your will. Only if success comes from You can it be enjoyed.

CALL ON THE
NAME OF THE LORD

"Isaac built an altar there and called on the name of the LORD. There he pitched his tent, and there his servants dug a well."

GENESIS 26:25

LORD, You are the God of the universe and Lord of my life. I worship You and give glory to Your name. You are holy and wonderful—amazing and awesome—and I thank You for all You have done for me. Because Your Word says You are able to do beyond what I can even think of to ask for, I call on You to meet all of my needs in ways more wonderful than I can even imagine. I have dug a place deep in my heart for Your living water to continuously flow.

Struggling in Prayer

"Jacob was left alone, and a man wrestled with him till daybreak. When the man saw that he could not overpower him, he touched the socket of Jacob's hip so that his hip was wrenched as he wrestled with the man. Then the man said, 'Let me go, for it is daybreak.' But Jacob replied, 'I will not let you go unless you bless me.'"

GENESIS 32:24-26

LORD, I desire to know You better so that I can experience all the blessings You have for me. I confess I don't pray as much as I would like to, and I have times of fear and doubt. But I commit this day to trust You more and to pray without ceasing—even if it feels like a struggle—because I know I will find transformation in Your presence. I will continue to reach for You until I sense the comfort of Your Holy Spirit.

THE POWER OF PRAISE

"Then come, let us go up to Bethel, where I will build an altar to God, who answered me in the day of my distress and who has been with me wherever I have gone."

GENESIS 35:3

ALMIGHTY GOD, I worship You for who You are. I thank You for all You have done for me. You have given me strength, power, provision, and purpose. I know I need not fear the future because I see how You have blessed me and protected me in the past. I pray You will always guide me in the way I should go. I praise You for Your presence and Your promise to never forsake me.

Praying for
Your Children

"Then he blessed Joseph and said, 'May the God before whom my fathers Abraham and Isaac walked, the God who has been my shepherd all my life to this day, the Angel who has delivered me from all harm—may he bless these boys. May they be called by my name and the names of my fathers Abraham and Isaac, and may they increase greatly upon the earth.'"

Genesis 48:15-16

Heavenly Father, teach me to pray for my children and grandchildren and any children You put in my life. Bless each child with a knowledge of who You are and help them to live Your way so they can stay on the path You have for their lives. Enable each child to recognize the gifts and talents You have put in them, and to follow Your leading as they develop and use them for Your glory.

CRYING OUT TO GOD

*"During that long period, the king of Egypt
died. The Israelites groaned in their slavery
and cried out, and their cry for help because
of their slavery went up to God."*

EXODUS 2:23

LORD, I cry out to You for deliverance from anything that keeps me from becoming all You created me to be. Set me free from everything that separates me from You. Lord, I know that even in the midst of what seems to be the most hopeless situation, You can do Your greatest work. Thank You that You are a God of miracles. I pray You will do a miracle in my life today.

Praying on Behalf of Others

*"Pharaoh quickly summoned Moses and Aaron and said, 'I have sinned against the L*ORD *your God and against you. Now forgive my sin once more and pray to the L*ORD *your God to take this deadly plague away from me.'"*

EXODUS 10:16-17

GOD, help me to learn to pray in power. Increase my faith to believe for the answers to my prayers. Enable me to become an intercessor for others—especially those who do not know You. I pray that everyone around me will be able to recognize by my life that I am a person of great faith and power in prayer, and that they can trust in the God to whom I pray.

Praying Against
a Hard Heart

*"Then the Lord said to Moses, 'Go to Pharaoh,
for I have hardened his heart and the hearts
of his officials so that I may perform these
miraculous signs of mine among them.'"*

Exodus 10:1

Lord, I pray my heart will never become hard toward You or Your ways, or toward others either. Keep me far from pride or arrogance. Help me to never neglect to glorify You and give You thanks and praise for all You have done in the world and in my life. Help me to always stay softhearted toward You and to remain open to Your leading and Your will for me. Help me to rely on Your strength and power and not my own.

Stop Praying
and Start Moving

"Then the Lord said to Moses, 'Why are you crying out to me? Tell the Israelites to move on.'"

Exodus 14:15

Holy Father, help me to understand—as I am in prayer and waiting for a leading from You—when it is time to take action. Help me to be wise enough to recognize the answers to my prayers when they come in ways I was not expecting. Give me the knowledge of Your will that lets me know when it is time to stand up and take steps of faith.

THE POWER OF
LITTLE BY LITTLE

"Little by little I will drive them out before
you, until you have increased enough
to take possession of the land."

EXODUS 23:30

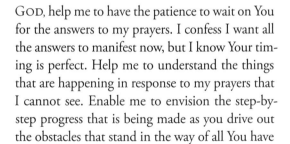

GOD, help me to have the patience to wait on You for the answers to my prayers. I confess I want all the answers to manifest now, but I know Your timing is perfect. Help me to understand the things that are happening in response to my prayers that I cannot see. Enable me to envision the step-by-step progress that is being made as you drive out the obstacles that stand in the way of all You have for my life.

THE POWER OF INTERCESSION

*"Then the LORD relented and did not bring on
his people the disaster he had threatened."*

EXODUS 32:14

LORD, help me to have a greater knowledge of Your
Word so that I can always pray in alignment with
Your will. I know the power I have in prayer is Your
power working through me. Help me to never get
in the way of what You want to do in response to
my prayers. Help me to make a major difference in
the lives of my family, friends, and neighbors when
I pray. Thank You for Your mercy that spares us
from the consequences we deserve.

Why We Do What We Do

"Aaron's sons Nadab and Abihu took their censers, put fire in them and added incense; and they offered unauthorized fire before the LORD, contrary to his command. So fire came out from the presence of the LORD and consumed them, and they died before the LORD."

LEVITICUS 10:1-2

HOLY FATHER, help me to never be careless about Your ways or Your Word. Enable me to not allow anything that has to do with my worship of You to become lifeless or like a ritual that has lost its depth of meaning. Keep the disciplines of prayer, praise, and reading in Your Word fresh and alive in my heart so that I will always have a passionate hunger for Your presence.

Your Day of Atonement

*"On that day the priest shall make atonement for you,
to cleanse you, that you may be clean
from all your sins before the Lord."*

Leviticus 16:30 nkjv

Thank You, Jesus, for paying the price for my sins so that I don't have to. Because of You I have been reconciled to God, and I will never be separated from Him again. Help me to extend to others the love and forgiveness You've given to me. Teach me ways I can bless You and show my gratitude to You for all You have done.

How Can I Be Holy?

*"Speak to the entire assembly of Israel
and say to them: 'Be holy because
I, the LORD your God, am holy.'"*

LEVITICUS 19:2

DEAR GOD, I worship You for Your greatness and goodness. I praise You for Your holiness. As I worship You, I pray Your holiness will rub off on me. Help me to take on the beauty of Your holiness as I spend time in Your presence. Enable me to become more like You so that Your holiness will make me whole. I pray that Your Spirit in me will be a light that draws others to You.

THE ACT OF CELEBRATION

*"Speak to the Israelites and say to them:
'These are my appointed feasts, the
appointed feasts of the LORD, which you
are to proclaim as sacred assemblies.'"*

LEVITICUS 23:2

DEAR LORD, I celebrate the moment when I came to know You as my Lord. I celebrate the times You have healed me and blessed me. I celebrate Your answers to my prayers and the times You saved me from my own mistakes. I celebrate the wonderful people You have put in my life—especially the ones who have led me to You and taught me to live Your way. I celebrate my life with You.

THE IMPORTANCE
OF RESTITUTION

*"When a man or woman wrongs another in
any way and so is unfaithful to the LORD,
that person is guilty and must confess the
sin he has committed. He must make full
restitution for his wrong, add one fifth to it
and give it all to the person he has wronged."*

NUMBERS 5:6-7

GOD, I pray You would show me if I have hurt anyone in any way. If I have, show me how I can make it up to them so that things are right between us. Help me to apologize and to ask for that person's forgiveness. Help me to have a pure heart, righteous thoughts, and good motives. I want to always have a clear conscience so that nothing will undermine the closeness I have with You.

GUIDANCE FOR THE JOURNEY

"Whenever the cloud lifted from above the Tent, the Israelites set out; wherever the cloud settled, the Israelites encamped...
At the LORD's command they encamped, and at the LORD's command they set out. They obeyed the LORD's order, in accordance with his command through Moses."

NUMBERS 9:17,23

LORD, guide me on my journey through life. Help me to understand and recognize Your leading in every decision I make. Give me clear direction so that I can stay on the path You have for me. I know following You doesn't mean everything will be easy. Help me to not lose faith when the road gets rough. I want to always arrive at the place You want me to be.

When You're Feeling Overwhelmed

"I will come down and speak with you there, and I will take of the Spirit that is on you and put the Spirit on them. They will help you carry the burden of the people so that you will not have to carry it alone."

NUMBERS 11:17

GOD, I lift up to You the areas of my life that are overwhelming and burdensome. I have not come to You to complain, but rather to seek Your help. Where I have tried to handle everything in my own strength instead of depending on You, I ask Your forgiveness. I pray You will take each burden of my heart and enable me to rise above every challenging situation in my life.

PRAYING FOR THOSE WHO HAVE HURT YOU

*"If you forgive men their trespasses,
your heavenly Father will also forgive you."*

MATTHEW 6:14 NKJV

LORD, I pray You would help me to forgive anyone who has hurt me. Enable me to forgive them so completely that I don't hesitate to pray for their greatest blessing. Deliver me from any bitterness, and help me to live in the freedom of a forgiving heart so that there is complete reconciliation between us. I don't want to experience the terrible consequences of unforgiveness in my life. I want to be free to receive all the healing and wholeness You have for me.

Just Enough Light for the Step You're On

"'In accordance with your great love, forgive the sin of these people, just as you have pardoned them from the time they left Egypt until now.' The LORD replied, 'I have forgiven them, as you asked.'"

NUMBERS 14:19-20

DEAR GOD, just as you walked with Your people in the desert after You delivered them out of Egypt, and You forgave them and provided what they needed every step of the way, I turn to You for deliverance and forgiveness and ask that You would provide for my needs every day. Help me to never doubt that You will always give me the light I need for each step I take.

The Power of Faith

"The people came to Moses and said, 'We sinned when we spoke against the LORD and against you. Pray that the LORD will take the snakes away from us.' So Moses prayed for the people. The LORD said to Moses, 'Make a snake and put it up on a pole; anyone who is bitten can look at it and live.'"

NUMBERS 21:7-8

LORD JESUS, I look to You as my Savior and to what You accomplished on the cross as the guarantee of my salvation. Thank You for paying the price for my sin. Forgive me if I have ever spoken against You in any way, or have been motivated by fear and doubt. I come to You in faith, believing that You hear me and will answer my prayer. Help me to always obey You and avoid the consequences of disobedience.

BE CAREFUL
WHAT YOU PROMISE

*"This is what the LORD commands: When a man
made a vow to the LORD or takes an oath to
obligate himself by a pledge, he must not break
his word but must do everything he said."*

NUMBERS 30:1-2

GOD, I pray You would help me to always honor
my word and keep my promises. Give me the wisdom to not promise something I cannot do or give.
Where I have already given my word or said I would
do something and have not done it, help me to
make the amends necessary to rectify that. Where I
have vowed to do something for You, enable me to
do all that I have said.

DO NOT BE AFRAID

"See, the LORD your God has given you the land. Go up and take possession of it as the LORD, the God of your fathers, told you. Do not be afraid; do not be discouraged."

DEUTERONOMY 1:21

THANK YOU, Lord, for all the wonderful things You have done for me in the *past*, that You are doing for me *today*, and that You *will* do for me in the *future*. Keep me from fear and discouragement as I look at the challenges ahead. Thank You that You go before me with a plan for battle. I look to You for guidance so I may possess all You have for me.

GOD IS NEAR
WHEN WE PRAY

"What other nation is so great as to have their gods near them the way the LORD our God is near us whenever we pray to him?"

DEUTERONOMY 4:7

LORD, I thank You for being close to me when I pray. Thank You that You hear and will answer me. Thank You that in Your presence there is transformation for my soul and my life. I draw close to You now and ask for an ever-increasing sense of Your presence. I ask that You would help me to pray more and more every day and give me increasing faith to believe for the answers.

PRAYERS OF INTERCESSION

"I feared the anger and wrath of the LORD, for
he was angry enough with you to destroy you.
But again the LORD listened to me. And the
LORD was angry enough with Aaron to destroy
him, but at that time I prayed for Aaron too."

DEUTERONOMY 9:19-20

GOD, help me to be one of Your faithful and powerful intercessors. Help me to not be so focused on myself and my situation that I don't see how to pray for the needs of others. Give me strong faith to believe that my prayers can make a big difference in their lives. Show me the people I need to pray for today and how I should specifically pray for them.

GOD IS WITH YOU

*"When you go to war against your enemies
and see horses and chariots and an army
greater than yours, do not be afraid of them,
because the LORD your God, who brought
you up out of Egypt, will be with you."*

DEUTERONOMY 20:1

ALMIGHTY GOD, I rely on You to lead me through
every challenge and battle in my life. Help me to
never operate out of fear in the face of what seem
like impossible circumstances. Just as You have
helped me in the past, I know You will continue
to help me in the future. I praise You for the great
things You will do, and thank You that Your presence is always with me.

Praise God for His Greatness

"I will proclaim the name of the Lord. Oh, praise the greatness of our God! He is the Rock, his works are perfect, and all his ways are just. A faithful God who does no wrong, upright and just is he."

Deuteronomy 32:3-4

God, I praise You for Your greatness and goodness. I worship You as the God of creation and the Lord of my life. I praise You in the good times and in the difficult times as well. Thank You that You show Your love for me by protecting me, providing for me, delivering me, and giving me Your peace and power. You are greater than anything I face.

GOD IS YOUR REFUGE

"There is no one like the God of Jeshurun, who rides on the heavens to help you and on the clouds in his majesty. The eternal God is your refuge, and underneath are the everlasting arms…Blessed are you, O Israel! Who is like you, a people saved by the LORD? He is your shield and helper and your glorious sword."

DEUTERONOMY 33:26-27,29

LORD, You are great and there is no other God but You. You are my safe refuge from the storm. Help me to find my rest in You as You go to battle against all that opposes me. No matter whether my battles are with finances, relationships, health, or obedience, I know that because of Your presence in my life, I will never face those challenges alone. I depend on Your strength and not mine.

Looking for God's Will

"Do not let this Book of the Law depart from your mouth; meditate on it day and night, so that you may be careful to do everything written in it. Then you will be prosperous and successful."

JOSHUA 1:8

DEAR LORD, I pray that every time I read Your Word, You will teach me all I need to know. Help me to understand Your truth and speak to me specifically about how each passage I have read relates to my life and to the lives of others. Help me to meditate on Your Word and take steps of obedience so that I can live in Your perfect will and prosper as You have promised.

LOOKING FOR
A BREAKTHROUGH?

*"When the trumpets sounded, the people shouted,
and at the sound of the trumpet, when the people
gave a loud shout, the wall collapsed; so every
man charged straight in, and they took the city."*

JOSHUA 6:20

FATHER GOD, I depend on You to help me overcome the obstacles in my life. Teach me to speak Your Word in power as I cover each situation in prayer. I lift up praise to You in the face of impossible circumstances because You are the God of the impossible. No matter what comes against me, Your power is more than enough to break through that to victory.

ROADBLOCKS TO PRAYER

*"The LORD said to Joshua, 'Stand up! What
are you doing down on your face? Israel
has sinned; they have violated my covenant,
which I commanded them to keep.'"*

JOSHUA 7:10-11

LORD, I know my prayers have no effect if I have
sin in my life for which I have not repented or confessed. Reveal to me any sin I am harboring, and
I will confess it so that nothing comes between
You and me. I don't want to give place to any hindrances to my prayers, and I don't want to put up a
roadblock to all You want to do in my life.

Inquire of the Lord

*"The men of Israel sampled their provisions
but did not inquire of the LORD."*

Joshua 9:14

Father, I pray You would help me to not run off on my own, trying to do what I *think* is right, instead of inquiring of You about everything so that I will do what I *know* is right. Help me to not fall into the traps the enemy has laid for me by forgetting to consult You about everything—even the things I may think I can handle on my own. Help me to pray about everything and seek Your guidance in all matters.

Get Personal with God

*"Therefore the Lord was very angry with
Israel and said, 'Because this nation has
violated the covenant that I laid down for
their forefathers and has not listened to me,
I will no longer drive out before them any
of the nations Joshua left when he died.'"*

Judges 2:20-21

Father God, I don't want to ever fall away from
You by neglecting to spend time in Your Word
and in prayer. I want to always be gaining a closer
walk with You. Help me to know You better and
to become more and more like You. Enable me to
resist temptation, sin, or laziness. Teach me how to
listen to You directing me so I can have a new and
deeper experience with You every day.

God Delivers

"But when they cried out to the Lord, he raised up for them a deliverer, Othniel son of Kenaz, Caleb's younger brother, who saved them…Again the Israelites cried out to the Lord, and he gave them a deliverer—Ehud, a left-handed man, the son of Gera the Benjamite."

Judges 3:9,15

Dear Lord, I pray that wherever the enemy has erected a stronghold in my life for my destruction, You would deliver me from it. Thank You that You paid the price for my freedom and You continue to set me free every day. I lift You up, exalt You, and praise You as my Savior and Deliverer. I am grateful that when I cry out to You, You set me free.

Confession
and Repentance

*"But the Israelites said to the LORD, 'We have
sinned. Do with us whatever you think best, but
please rescue us now.' Then they got rid of the
foreign gods among them and served the LORD.
And he could bear Israel's misery no longer."*

Judges 10:15-16

DEAR GOD, I don't want anything to separate me
from You. Nothing is worth that. I want to confess to You anything I have done wrong, and anything that is not pleasing in Your eyes. Wherever I
have worshipped other gods or harbored what You
would consider an idol in my life, reveal it to me
and I will confess it, repent of it, and get rid of it. I
want to serve only You.

43

Know the Source

*"He told them what Micah had done for him
and said, 'He has hired me and I am his
priest.' Then they said to him, 'Please inquire
of God to learn whether our journey will be
successful.' The priest answered them, 'Go in
peace. Your journey has the LORD's approval.'"*

JUDGES 18:4-6

LORD, I turn to You for all wisdom, direction, and guidance. Where I must seek advice from another person, help me to know when that person speaks from godly knowledge and when this is not the case. Help me to always test the input of others with Your Word. I want You to be my ultimate source for all knowledge. I want to be certain that the path I am walking has Your approval.

Be Careful
What You Ask For

*"So all the elders of Israel gathered together
and came to Samuel at Ramah. They said
to him, 'You are old, and your sons do not
walk in your ways; now appoint a king to
lead us, such as all the other nations have.'"*

1 Samuel 8:4-5

Help me, Holy Spirit of God, to walk in Your ways.
Speak to me as I read Your Word so that I can grow
in understanding. Enable me to pray in power and
alignment with what pleases You. Thank You for
the times I prayed for something and You didn't
give it to me because You were keeping me on the
right path. Help me not to seek after what other
people have, but rather to want only what *You* have
for me.

GIVE THE GIFT OF PRAYER

"As for me, far be it from me that I should sin against the LORD by failing to pray for you. And I will teach you the way that is good and right."

1 SAMUEL 12:23

LORD, I pray for each member of my family and for all of my friends and acquaintances to be blessed with peace, good health, provision, and a greater knowledge of You and Your Word. Help me to not be selfish or lazy in my praying. Show me specifically who else I need to pray for. May I never sin against You by failing to pray for people You have put in my life.

GOD LOOKS
ON YOUR HEART

*"But the LORD said to Samuel, 'Do not consider
his appearance or his height, for I have rejected
him. The LORD does not look at the things
man looks at. Man looks at the outward
appearance, but the LORD looks at the heart.'"*

1 SAMUEL 16:7

DEAR LORD, I am grateful that You do not judge
me the way people do. Thank You that You look on
my heart to see my thoughts, attitudes, and love
for You, and not how successful or attractive I am.
Show me anything in my heart that should not be
there, and I will confess it before You. Remove all
selfish and sinful desires and fill my heart with Your
love, peace, and joy. Give me a heart that pleases
You.

WHEN GOD
DOESN'T ANSWER

"He inquired of the LORD, but the LORD did not answer him by dreams or Urim or prophets."

1 SAMUEL 28:6

GOD, I thank You that You always hear my prayers. Give me patience to wait for the answers to come in Your way and in Your perfect timing. Give me peace to accept Your answer—even if it is no. Help me to never take matters into my own hands to try to make something happen that is not Your will. I trust that You know what is best for me at all times.

When God Gives
Specific Instructions

"So David inquired of the Lord, 'Shall I go and attack the Philistines? Will you hand them over to me?' The Lord answered him, 'Go, for I will surely hand the Philistines over to you.'"

2 Samuel 5:19

Lord, I don't want to take one step or make any decision without Your leading. I know You care about even the smallest details of my life and want to guide me in the way I should go. Take away my peace if I should decide to step off the path of Your greatest blessing for my life. Give me instructions so that I never stray from Your perfect will.

WHEN GOD SAYS NO

"Go and tell my servant David, 'This is what the
LORD says: Are you the one to build me a house to
dwell in?... When your days are over and you rest
with your fathers, I will raise up your offspring
to succeed you, who will come from your own
body, and I will establish his kingdom. He is the
one who will build a house for my Name, and I
will establish the throne of his kingdom forever.'"

2 SAMUEL 7:5,12-13

∽

DEAR LORD, just as Your servant David wanted to
build Your temple, but You told him no, help me
to accept Your answers to my prayers, even when
the answer is not what I want. Enable me to always
understand Your will, especially when the answers
to my prayers are not what I expected. I am grateful that You know what is best for me and will keep
me from seeking after things I shouldn't.

The Quicksand of Temptation

"One evening David got up from his bed and walked around on the roof of the palace. From the roof he saw a woman bathing. The woman was very beautiful, and David sent someone to find out about her."

2 SAMUEL 11:2-3

DEAR GOD, I pray You will help me to always successfully resist temptation from the moment I am confronted with it. Help me to draw *closer* to You when anything tries to draw me *away*. Deliver me from the trap of temptation before I fall into it. Give me the strength, wisdom, and knowledge I need to fully resist temptation at all times.

THE IMPORTANCE
OF CONFESSION

*"David was conscience-stricken after he had
counted the fighting men, and he said to the
LORD, 'I have sinned greatly in what I have done.
Now, O LORD, I beg you, take away the guilt of
your servant. I have done a very foolish thing.'"*

2 SAMUEL 24:10

LORD, I pray You would show me any sin in my
life so that I can confess it before You. I don't want
guilt in my conscience to dilute my walk with You
or inhibit my prayers because I am ashamed to come
before You in confidence. Help me to always have a
repentant heart before You so that I will quickly turn
away from sin. Keep me from doing foolish things.

HUMBLED IN HIS PRESENCE

"But will God really dwell on earth? The heavens,
even the highest heaven, cannot contain you.
How much less this temple I have built!"

1 KINGS 8:27

DEAR LORD, I thank You for Your presence in my life. I am thankful and humbled that You—through Your Holy Spirit—live inside me. Help me to never be full of myself, but rather to always be freshly filled with more of You each day. Help me to have a sense of Your presence, especially as I read Your Word and pray and live in obedience to Your ways.

PUTTING GOD
ABOVE ALL ELSE

"As Solomon grew old, his wives turned his heart after other gods, and his heart was not fully devoted to the LORD his God, as the heart of David his father had been."

1 KINGS 11:4

GOD, I pray my treasure will always be in You and not in my possessions or the distractions of this world. Help me to never make an idol out of anything or anyone, or put them before You in any way. I give You honor and gratitude for all the good things You have given me. You are my greatest desire, and I put You above all else in my life.

LEARNING TO PRAY BOLDLY

"Go and tell Hezekiah, 'Thus says the LORD...
"I have heard your prayer, I have seen your tears;
surely I will add to your days fifteen years."'"

1 KINGS 17:1

LORD, I know You are the God of miracles and nothing is impossible for those who pray in the power of Your Spirit. Help me to pray boldly and believe for miracles in answer to my prayers. Teach me how to not pray too small. I don't want my prayers to stop short of what You want to see happen in my life and in the lives of those for whom I pray.

EXPECTANT PRAYER

"Answer me, O LORD, answer me, so these people
will know that you, O LORD, are God, and
that you are turning their hearts back again.'
Then the fire of the LORD fell and burned up
the sacrifice, the wood, the stones and the soil,
and also licked up the water in the trench."

1 KINGS 18:37-38

DEAR LORD, I pray You would help me to have strong faith to believe You will do great things in response to my prayers. Your Word tells of the magnificent and miraculous things You have done for people, and I know You are the same today and in the future as You were in the past. Turn my heart toward You so that my expectations are always in Your goodness.

GOD WILL POUR OUT AS MUCH AS YOU CAN RECEIVE

"Elisha said, 'Go around and ask all your neighbors for empty jars. Don't ask for just a few. Then go inside and shut the door behind you and your sons. Pour oil into all the jars, and as each is filled, put it to one side.'"

2 KINGS 4:3-4

HEAVENLY FATHER, give me a vision of all You want to do in my life. Help me to not think too small, even when I pray. I want to be available to whatever You have for me and not limit Your blessings by being unprepared to receive them. Enlarge my heart and mind to understand how You can take what I have and expand it beyond what I can imagine. Pour out on me all I can contain.

Open My Eyes, Lord

"And Elisha prayed, 'O LORD, open his eyes so he may see.' Then the LORD opened the servant's eyes, and he looked and saw the hills full of horses and chariots of fire all around Elisha. As the enemy came down toward him, Elisha prayed to the LORD, 'Strike these people with blindness.' So he struck them with blindness, as Elisha had asked."

2 KINGS 6:17-18

ALMIGHTY GOD, I pray You would open my eyes to see the truth about my situation. Give me clear understanding—especially when I am facing the enemy—of all You are doing in the midst of my situation. Help me to trust Your hand of protection. Enable me to see things from Your perspective so that I can stand strong. Teach me to pray according to Your will.

Undeserved
Answers to Prayer

*"You our God have punished us less
than our iniquities deserve."*

Ezra 9:13 NKJV

Dear Lord, I thank You that You hear my prayers and answer, not according to my own goodness, but according to Yours. Help me to not let anything discourage me from coming to You in prayer—especially not my own sense that I am undeserving of Your attention and blessing. I come before You entirely because You are full of grace and mercy.

An Undivided Heart

"They worshiped the LORD, but they also appointed all sorts of their own people to officiate for them as priests in the shrines at the high places. They worshiped the LORD, but they also served their own gods in accordance with the customs of the nations from which they had been brought."

2 Kings 17:32-33

DEAR GOD, I pray You would keep me from ever having a divided heart. I don't want to weaken my allegiance to You by showing any allegiance to the false gods of this world. Help me to stay in close touch with You through constant and fervent prayer. Unite my heart with Yours so that it never strays.

REMEMBER ME, LORD

"Hezekiah turned his face to the wall and prayed to the LORD, 'Remember, O LORD, how I have walked before you faithfully and with wholehearted devotion and have done what is good in your eyes.' And Hezekiah wept bitterly."

2 KINGS 20:2-3

LORD, You are my Healer and Deliverer. In times of sickness, injury, or affliction, I pray You would remember me and heal me from anything that would threaten to diminish or end my life. Help me to be able to serve You longer and ever more effectively and not succumb to the plans of the enemy for my demise. Remember me with Your gift of renewed health and wholeness.

Be Bold to Ask

"Jabez cried out to the God of Israel, 'Oh, that you would bless me and enlarge my territory! Let your hand be with me, and keep me from harm so that I will be free from pain.' And God granted his request."

1 Chronicles 4:10

GOD, I thank You for all You have given me. I pray for Your continued blessings, provision, and protection. Thank You that You are pleased to share Yourself and Your kingdom with me. I pray Your presence will always be with me wherever I go and no matter what happens. Enable me to give back to You by helping and blessing others.

Pray Before You Act

"Now the Philistines had come and raided the Valley of Rephaim; so David inquired of God: 'Shall I go and attack the Philistines? Will you hand them over to me?' The LORD answered him, 'Go, I will hand them over to you.'"

1 Chronicles 14:9-10

DEAR LORD, help me to always inquire of You first before I take action. I don't want to assume that because You instructed me in a certain way before, You will instruct me in the same way each time I am faced with a similar situation. I don't want to mistakenly think I have all the answers when only You have all the answers for my life. Enable me to remember to seek You in everything I do.

God Does More Than You Can Imagine

"And now, LORD, let the promise you have made concerning your servant and his house be established forever. Do as you promised, so that it will be established and that your name will be great forever. Then men will say, 'The LORD Almighty, the God over Israel, is Israel's God!' And the house of your servant David will be established before you."

1 Chronicles 17:23-24

❧

LORD, I confess any disappointment I have had when my prayers were not answered the way I wanted them to be. I know my greatest blessing will come about because of Your will being done in my life. I also know that what You have for me is far greater than what I can imagine for myself. Forgive me for any time I did not trust that to be true. Establish my footsteps securely on the path You have for me.

Repenting Before God in Prayer

*"David said to God, 'Was it not I who ordered
the fighting men to be counted? I am the one
who has sinned and done wrong. These are but
sheep. What have they done? O LORD my God,
let your hand fall upon me and my family, but
do not let this plague remain on your people.'"*

1 Chronicles 21:17

LORD, I see in Your Word the terrible consequences
of pride. I don't want to experience those consequences in my life, and I especially don't want to
have my family suffer because of my sin. Reveal any
pride in me so that I can confess and repent of it
before You immediately. Help me to always have a
humble heart, so that I will live my life Your way.

The Power of
Praise-Filled Giving

*"Wealth and honor come from you; you
are the ruler of all things. In your hands
are strength and power to exalt and give
strength to all. Now, our God, we give you
thanks, and praise your glorious name."*

1 Chronicles 29:12-13

Heavenly Father, I thank You and praise You
for all You have given me. Help me to give back
to You with the same heart of praise I have when I
receive from You. I want to be a cheerful giver. Help
me to never value my possessions more than I value
You and Your laws. Enable me to give the way You
want me to, beginning with my worship of You.

INVITING GOD'S PRESENCE AND FORGIVENESS

"Now, my God, may your eyes be open and your
ears attentive to the prayers offered in this place.
Now arise, O LORD God, and come to your resting
place, you and the ark of your might. May your
priests, O LORD God, be clothed with salvation,
may your saints rejoice in your goodness."

2 CHRONICLES 6:40-41

HOLY FATHER, there is nothing more important than Your presence in my life. Help me to be a holy place for Your Spirit to dwell. Forgive me of all sin and cleanse my heart of all unrighteousness. Nothing is more comforting to me than to know You are with me, no matter what is happening in my life. I rejoice in Your unfailing goodness toward me.

Why We Must Pray
for Our Nation

*"If my people, who are called by my name, will
humble themselves and pray and seek my
face and turn from their wicked ways, then
will I hear from heaven and will forgive
their sin and will heal their land."*

2 Chronicles 7:14

Lord God, I come humbly before You and confess the sins of my nation. I pray we as a people
would turn from our wicked ways and seek Your
face so that You will hear our prayers, forgive our
sins, and heal our land. We desperately need Your
hand of blessing and protection upon our country. Pour out Your Spirit on us and work Your righteousness in the hearts of the people.

Move in the Power of God

"The eyes of the Lord run to and fro throughout the whole earth, to show Himself strong on behalf of those whose heart is loyal to Him."

2 Chronicles 16:9 nkjv

Lord, I am grateful for Your power extended to me. You have shown Yourself strong on my behalf countless times. By Your great and almighty power You have saved and redeemed me. You have delivered me, protected me, and provided for me, and I know You will continue to do so. You uphold all things by the word of Your power (Hebrews 1:3). Thank You that because You are all-powerful, that means all things are possible. Therefore I refuse to become discouraged or fearful about any aspect of my life. I will not trust in the wisdom of man, but I will trust in You and Your perfect wisdom and power.

Deliverance May Be Only a Prayer Away

"When the chariot commanders saw Jehoshaphat, they thought, 'This is the king of Israel.' So they turned to attack him, but Jehoshaphat cried out, and the LORD helped him. God drew them away from him."

2 Chronicles 18:31

LORD, I pray You would strengthen my faith so that I will not give up praying in the heat of the battle of opposition from the enemy. I realize the very next prayer I pray may be the one that will bring total deliverance from any strongholds the enemy is trying to erect in my life. Enable me to stand strong in prayer and worship, giving thanks that Your presence brings delivering power.

Even When We Don't Do Everything Right

"Although most of the many people who came from Ephraim, Manasseh, Issachar and Zebulun had not purified themselves, yet they ate the Passover, contrary to what was written. But Hezekiah prayed for them, saying, 'May the LORD, who is good, pardon everyone who sets his heart on seeking God—the LORD, the God of his fathers—even if he is not clean according to the rules of the sanctuary.' And the LORD heard Hezekiah and healed the people."

2 Chronicles 30:18-20

GOD, I thank You that even when I don't do everything right, You see in my heart the desire to do so, and You bless me anyway. I am grateful You look past my imperfections and see the perfect qualities of Your Son, Jesus, stamped on my heart instead. Help me to live Your way so that everything I do is pleasing to You and I receive the healing I need.

GOD IS ON YOUR SIDE

"'Be strong and courageous. Do not be afraid
or discouraged because of the king of Assyria
and the vast army with him, for there is a
greater power with us than with him. With
him is only the arm of flesh, but with us is
the LORD our God to help us and to fight our
battles.' And the people gained confidence from
what Hezekiah the king of Judah said."

2 CHRONICLES 32:7-8

THANK YOU, Lord, that You are with me in everything that I face. No matter what comes against me,
You are greater and more powerful. I ask You to be
with me in the things I struggle with today. I praise
You for Your greatness in the midst of all that seems
large and looming in my life. I worship You in the
middle of any enemy onslaught against me.

Praise God for His Love

"With praise and thanksgiving they sang to the LORD: 'He is good; his love to Israel endures forever.' And all the people gave a great shout of praise to the LORD, because the foundation of the house of the LORD was laid."

Ezra 3:11

LORD, I praise Your name. You are almighty and far above all things. Your presence and love in my life is greater than anything I fear. I know my faith in You and in Your Word will conquer all insecurity. With Your help, I will not dwell on my problems. Instead, I will praise You for Your goodness. Thank You for loving me.

THE DISCIPLINE OF FASTING WITH PRAYER

"So we fasted and petitioned our God about this, and he answered our prayer."

EZRA 8:23

LORD, help me to fast and pray regularly. Show me how often and how long and give me the strength to get through each fast successfully. With every fast, help me to pray powerfully about the issues of my life and the situations in my world. I want to deny my flesh so that I can exalt You above everything else in my life.

Be Watchful in Prayer

*"But we prayed to our God and posted a
guard day and night to meet this threat."*

Nehemiah 4:9

Dear God, I pray You would help me to be watchful in prayer so that I am always aware of what I am supposed to be doing, as well as clearly understanding what I am *not* to do. Help me to pray without ceasing so that I can stand guard against every plan of the enemy. I pray that You will be a guard over me to protect me from the things I cannot see.

THANK GOD FOR
HIS MERCY TO YOU

*"But in your great mercy you did not put
an end to them or abandon them, for you
are a gracious and merciful God."*

NEHEMIAH 9:31

LORD, I am aware every day of Your great mercy
toward me. Thank You that You have never judged
me according to what I have deserved. Your grace
toward me is beyond comprehension. Thank You
that You will never forsake me. Help me to not forsake You in any way either. I pray that my attitude
will always be right before You, and I will never take
Your mercy for granted.

The Power of Fasting and Prayer

"Go, gather together all the Jews who are in Susa, and fast for me. Do not eat or drink for three days, night or day. I and my maids will fast as you do. When this is done, I will go to the king, even though it is against the law. And if I perish, I perish."

ESTHER 4:16

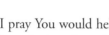

LORD, I pray You would help me to be a person like Esther, who has a heart for You and Your ways, and one who is in the right place at the right time. Enable me, whenever I fast and pray, to have a powerful effect on the world around me by standing up for what is right and following Your leading. Make my prayers powerful enough to save the lives of the people for whom I pray.

Praising God in Good Times and Bad

"At this, Job got up and tore his robe and shaved his head. Then he fell to the ground in worship and said: 'Naked I came from my mother's womb, and naked I will depart. The Lord gave and the Lord has taken away; may the name of the Lord be praised.'"

Job 1:20-21

Dear God, I will praise You no matter what is happening in my life—in good times and in bad times. Even in the midst of loss, disappointment, sickness, or failure, I lift up praise to You because I know every time I do, You will work powerfully in my situation and be glorified in the process. Help me to not become discouraged in the midst of struggle.

FACING YOUR FEARS

"What I feared has come upon me;
what I dreaded has happened to me.
I have no peace, no quietness;
I have no rest, but only turmoil."

Job 3:25-26

LORD, I lift up to You my deepest fears and ask that You would deliver me from them. Set me free from all dread and anxiety about the things that frighten me. Thank You that in Your presence all dread and anxiety is gone. Thank You that in the midst of Your perfect love, all fear in me is dissolved. You are greater than anything I face.

KNOWING GOD IS WITH YOU

*"What is man that you make so much of him,
that you give him so much attention?"*

JOB 7:17

HEAVENLY FATHER, it is hard to comprehend the depth of Your love for me and why You care about the details of my life. I am grateful that in difficult times You are with me, walking beside me all the way through to the other side of pain and trouble. Where bad things have happened and I have blamed You, I ask for Your forgiveness. Thank You for working things out for my good.

Finding Peace in the Midst of Suffering

"And these are but the outer fringe of his works;
how faint the whisper we hear of him! Who then
can understand the thunder of his power?"

Job 26:14

Almighty God, Your power is beyond comprehension. I can't begin to understand the far-reaching greatness of Your restoration and redemption in my life. Help me to never doubt You and Your ability to restore and redeem me. Help me to have such unwavering faith in the midst of difficult times that I rest in peace, knowing You will take care of all I care about.

FINDING A SONG
IN THE NIGHT

"But no one says, 'Where is God my
Maker, who gives songs in the night?'"

JOB 35:10

LORD, Your Word says that when we seek You, You will give us a song in the night. When I am going through a dark night of the soul, I pray You would enlighten my darkness with Your presence. In the face of the darkest situation in my life, I lift up songs of praise to You, knowing Your presence will inhabit them. Your light in me means I can never truly be in darkness.

GOD HEARS
WHEN YOU CALL

"Know that the LORD has set apart the godly for himself; the LORD will hear when I call to him."

PSALM 4:3

THANK YOU, Lord, that I am a child of Yours, set apart for Your glory, and that You hear my prayers. When I pray, help me to have the peace of knowing You have heard my prayer and will answer in Your way and in Your perfect timing. Show me if there is ever anything in my life that would become a barrier between me and You and cause my prayers to go unanswered.

PRAISE IS YOUR GREATEST WEAPON

"I will praise you, O LORD, with all my heart; I will tell of all your wonders...For he who avenges blood remembers; he does not ignore the cry of the afflicted."

PSALM 9:1,12

THANK YOU, God, that You never forget me. You always remember me and my situation, and You never ignore my cries to You when I am in need. I praise You in the middle of the struggles I face, knowing that worshipping You is my greatest weapon against the enemy of my soul. Help me to not just survive the attacks of the enemy, but to push the enemy back and crush him.

LOOK TO GOD AS
YOUR PROTECTOR

*"'Because of the oppression of the weak
and the groaning of the needy, I will
now arise,' says the Lord. 'I will protect
them from those who malign them.'"*

PSALM 12:5

Lord, I am grateful for all the times You have protected me from disaster. I'm sure there are countless ways You have kept me from harm that I am not even aware of. I pray You will always protect me and my reputation from anyone who would try to destroy me. Thank You that You hear my prayers for protection and You have promised to keep me safe.

Refuse to Give Up

*"I will bless the LORD who has given me counsel;
my heart also instructs me in the night seasons. I
have set the LORD always before me; because
He is at my right hand I shall not be moved."*

PSALM 16:7-8 NKJV

LORD, my hope is in You, and I know You will never fail me. Thank You that Your restoration is ongoing in my life. I am grateful that I am Your child and You have given me a purpose. Thank You for the great future You have for me because You love me. Thank You that I am never alone (Matthew 28:20). Help me to not think of giving up when things become difficult. Help me to remember that even in hard times You will help me persevere. Keep me from becoming discouraged in times of waiting. I know Your timing is perfect and the way You do things is right.

Persevering Prayer

*"You armed me with strength for battle; you
made my adversaries bow at my feet."*

Psalm 18:39

Lord, I am grateful that You have armed me with
the strength I need for the battle ahead. Help me
to subdue my enemies until they are completely
destroyed. Teach me to persevere in prayer and not
let down. Enable me to pray through each situation until I see victory over all opposition. Thank
You that You are always with me, working things
out in my favor.

IN THE CENTER
OF YOUR WILL

*"May He grant you according to your heart's
desire, and fulfill all your purpose."*

PSALM 20:4 NKJV

LORD, I commit my work to You. I pray that I will always be in Your will in whatever I do, and that I will do it well. I pray that all I do is pleasing to You and to those for whom and with whom I am working. Establish the work of my hands for Your pleasure and Your glory. Help me to understand what is the hope of my calling (Ephesians 1:17-18). Enable me to "be steadfast, immovable, always abounding in the work of the Lord" that You have given me to do, knowing that my "labor is not in vain in the Lord"—as long as it is *from* You and *for* You (1 Corinthians 15:58).

Your Heavenly Father Waits to Hear from You

"Though my father and mother forsake me, the LORD will receive me."

PSALM 27:10

DEAR HEAVENLY FATHER, I thank You that You will never forsake or desert me. Thank You that You always accept me. I am grateful for Your love, guidance, and comfort. Show me any place in my heart where I have not forgiven my own father or mother for letting me down in any way. I want to honor You by honoring them with complete forgiveness. Thank You for always hearing my prayers, just as a father listens to his child.

THE BLESSING
OF CONFESSING

*"Then I acknowledged my sin to you and
did not cover up my iniquity. I said, 'I will
confess my transgressions to the LORD'—
and you forgave the guilt of my sin."*

PSALM 32:5

DEAR LORD, I don't want anything to separate me
from You and all You have for me—especially not
my own unconfessed sin. I don't want to build a
wall between You and me by failing to acknowledge anything I thought, said, or did that was not
pleasing in Your sight. If I am too blind to see the
truth about myself, reveal it to me so that I can confess it before You.

LIVE IN THE FREEDOM GOD HAS FOR YOU

*"You are my hiding place; You shall preserve
me from trouble; You shall surround
me with songs of deliverance."*

PSALM 32:7 NKJV

LORD, I thank You that You are "my fortress, my high tower and my deliverer, my shield and the One in whom I take refuge" (Psalm 144:2). Show me anything I need to be set free from. I don't want to be living with something from which You already paid the price for me to be set free. I pray that You "will deliver me from every evil work and preserve me" for Your kingdom (2 Timothy 4:18). "O God, do not be far from me; O my God, make haste to help me!" (Psalm 71:12).

OVERFLOWING WITH JOY, PEACE, AND HOPE

*"Behold, the eye of the LORD is on those who
fear Him, on those who hope in His mercy."*

PSALM 33:18 NKJV

DEAR GOD, help me to resist the things that would
deplete my soul or minimize my strength. Fill me
instead with Your hope, peace, and joy, so much
so that they overflow from me to others. I praise
You for who You are and thank You that as I do,
Your Holy Spirit pours new life into me. Fill me
afresh with Your Spirit today and take all hopelessness away.

Make Worship a Habit

"I will bless the Lord at all times; His praise shall continually be in my mouth. My soul shall make its boast in the Lord; the humble shall hear of it and be glad."

Psalm 34:1-2 nkjv

Lord, I worship You as the almighty, all-powerful God of heaven and earth, and the Creator of all things. No one is greater than You. I praise You as my heavenly Father, who is with me every day to guide and protect me. Thank You for all You have given me, and all You will provide for me in the future. I praise You for Your love that liberates me and makes me whole. Pour Your love into me so that it overflows to others and glorifies You in the process.

REFUSE
NEGATIVE EMOTIONS

"The LORD redeems the soul of His servants, and none of those who trust in Him shall be condemned."

PSALM 34:22 NKJV

LORD, today I refuse all depression, anxiety, fear, dread, anger, and sadness, for I know they are not from You. By the power of Your Holy Spirit I resist the temptation to see the bad in life, and I ask You to open my eyes to the good. Enable me to sense Your presence at all times, no matter what is happening. My life is in Your hands, and Your love sustains me. May Your joy rise in my heart so fully that it crowds out all that is not of You. Enable me to breathe the fresh air of Your Spirit blowing the dark clouds away. Thank You that You are my light and You have forgiven me.

Letting Go of Things

"Blessed is he who considers the poor; the LORD will deliver him in time of trouble. The LORD will preserve him and keep him alive, and he will be blessed on the earth."

LORD, I don't want to stop up the flow of Your blessings in my life by not giving when and where I should. Help me to understand the release that happens in my life when I give so that I can let go of things. Help me to "not forget to do good and to share," for I know that with such sacrifices, You are well pleased. Help me to give and thereby store up treasures in heaven that do not fail, for I know that where my treasure is, my heart will be there also (Luke 12:33-34).

Pray to Resist
Temptation

*"Create in me a pure heart, O God, and renew
a steadfast spirit within me. Do not cast me
from your presence or take your Holy Spirit
from me. Restore to me the joy of your salvation
and grant me a willing spirit, to sustain me."*

PSALM 51:10-12

GOD, I pray You would create in me a clean and
right heart before You at all times. Help me to come
to You immediately at the very first sign of temptation so that I can stop any wrong thoughts from
turning into sinful actions. I don't want to ever be
separated from the presence of Your Holy Spirit.
Restore to me the joy I should always have because
of Your saving and redeeming love in my life.

Thirsting After God

"O God, you are my God, earnestly I seek you;
my soul thirsts for you, my body longs for you,
in a dry and weary land where there is no water."

Psalm 63:1

Lord God, more than anything else I want Your presence in my life. I long for more of You the way I long for water in the dry heat of summer. I come to You to quench my spiritual thirst as only You can do. Flow Your rivers of living water into me so they can revive my soul and then flow through me to a dry and thirsty world. Refresh me and renew my soul with Your healing presence.

Praying from a Right Heart

"If I had cherished sin in my heart, the Lord would not have listened; but God has surely listened and heard my voice in prayer. Praise be to God, who has not rejected my prayer or withheld his love from me!"

PSALM 66:18-20

LORD, I don't want to entertain sin in my heart. I want my heart to be right before You so that You will always hear my prayers. I know I don't do everything perfectly, so I ask that by the power of Your Holy Spirit You will enable me to keep my heart pure and my hands clean. Thank You for loving me and helping me do what is right in Your sight.

GOD'S POWER IN YOUR WEAKNESS

"God, You are more awesome than Your holy places. The God of Israel is He who gives strength and power to His people."

PSALM 68:35 NKJV

LORD, You give power to the weak and increase their strength (Isaiah 40:29). I thank You that I am the beneficiary of that. Help me to never forget Your power to redeem, save, restore, and renew. No matter what happens, I want to turn to You first and move in the power of Your Spirit. God of hope, help me to "abound in hope by the power of the Holy Spirit" (Romans 15:13). Thank You for the exceeding greatness of Your power toward those who believe (Ephesians 1:19). "For Yours is the power and the glory forever" (Matthew 6:13).

COMMIT YOUR
WORK TO GOD

*"May the favor of the Lord our God rest
upon us; establish the work of our hands for
us—yes, establish the work of our hands."*

PSALM 90:17

DEAR GOD, I pray You would bless my work and establish it. I commit all of the work I do to You so that it may be used for Your glory. Give me the strength to accomplish what I must do each day, and the wisdom and ability to do it well. Be in charge of every detail of my work so that it will find favor with others and be successful.

DELIVER ME, O LORD

"He shall call upon Me, and I will answer him;
I will be with him in trouble; I will deliver
him and honor him. With long life I will
satisfy him, and show him My salvation."

PSALM 91:15-16 NKJV

LORD, I see that the forces rising up against Your believers are powerful, but I know You are far more powerful than they are. Reveal to my heart Your power and might. I cry out to You to liberate me from the enemy who tries to put me into bondage. I thank You that You will answer by setting me free (Psalm 118:5). Thank You that You will never give up on me but will continue to deliver me (2 Corinthians 1:9-10). Thank You, Lord, that You will "deliver me from every evil work and preserve me" for Your heavenly kingdom.

YOU PROTECT ME, LORD

"He preserves the souls of His saints; He delivers them out of the hand of the wicked."

PSALM 97:10 NKJV

LORD, I thank You that You have delivered me from my enemy. Thank You, Jesus, that You came to "destroy the works of the devil" and You have already won the battle. I know that "though I walk in the midst of trouble, You will revive me; You will stretch out Your hand against the wrath of my enemies, and Your right hand will save me" (Psalm 138:7). Help me to "be wise in what is good, and simple concerning evil" for I know that You, the God of peace, "will crush Satan" under my feet quickly" (Romans 16:19-20).

EXPERIENCING THE POWER OF PRAISE

*"Enter his gates with thanksgiving
and his courts with praise."*

PSALM 100:4

LORD, I come before You with praise and thanksgiving for all that You are and everything You have done for me. No matter what happens in my life or in the world around me, I will not sink to the level of the problem. I will rise above my limitations by the power of Your Spirit and praise You as the solution to all my problems.

PRAISE IS THE PRAYER THAT CHANGES EVERYTHING

*"Hear my prayer, O LORD; let my cry for help
come to you. Do not hide your face from
me when I am in distress. Turn your ear
to me; when I call, answer me quickly."*

PSALM 102:1-2

DEAR GOD, I worship You and thank You that You
are greater than anything I face. Thank You that
You are a compassionate God of mercy and You
hear my prayers and answer them. I thank You that
You inhabit my praise, and that in Your presence
my life and circumstances are changed. I am grateful that praising You changes me.

Fear God, but Don't Live in Fear

"As a father has compassion on his children, so the
Lord has compassion on those who fear him."

Psalm 103:13

Lord, I bring all my fears to You and ask You to take them from me so that I no longer live in fear of anything. I know You have not given me a spirit of fear; You have given me love, power, and a sound mind. In Your presence all my fear is gone, for Your love takes it away. Help me to give the glory due You at all times, for I worship and praise You above all else. Enlarge my faith to extinguish all fear, so that the only fear I have is deep reverence of You.

RECOGNIZE YOUR ENEMY

*"Let the redeemed of the LORD say so, whom He
has redeemed from the hand of the enemy."*

PSALM 107:2 NKJV

LORD, keep me aware of when the enemy is attacking. Help me to be strong in Your Word and continuously in prayer so that I will not be caught off guard. Help me to never "give place to the devil" with disobedience to Your ways (Ephesians 4:27). Help me instead to submit to You and resist the devil so that he will flee from me. Enable me to stay in Your will so that I never come out from under the umbrella of Your protection. Teach me to make worship of You my first reaction to enemy attack. I praise You, Lord, for You have "delivered me out of all trouble; and my eye has seen its desire upon my enemies" (Psalm 54:7).

God Hears You
When You Pray

"I love the LORD, for he heard my voice; he heard
my cry for mercy. Because he turned his ear
to me, I will call on him as long as I live."

PSALM 116:1-2

LORD, I take great comfort in knowing You hear my prayers. Your Word tells me You listen and are never so far away that You cannot hear when I call. Help me to be patient to wait for Your answers, to not lose heart or fear that You have not heard. Help me to trust You every day of my life for as long as I live.

Take God at His Word

"I will worship toward Your holy temple and praise Your name, for Your lovingkindness and Your truth; for You have magnified Your word above all Your name."

PSALM 138:2 NKJV

LORD, I am grateful for Your Word. It shows me how to live, and I realize my life only works if I'm living Your way. Meet me there in the pages and teach me what I need to know. "Open my eyes that I may see wondrous things from Your law" (Psalm 119:18). Thank You for the comfort, healing, deliverance, and peace Your Word brings me. It is food for my starving soul. Help me to read it every day so that I have a solid understanding of who You are, who You made me to be, and how I am to live.

DELIVERED AND SET FREE

*"In the day when I cried out, You answered me,
and made me bold with strength in my soul."*

PSALM 138:3 NKJV

LORD, help me to see anything I dread as a challenge that I can rise above, because You enable me. You have brought me out of darkness and the shadow of death, and broke my chains of bondage. You have delivered me from darkness and brought me into Your kingdom and Your love (Colossians 1:13). Because You are my salvation, I don't have to be afraid. I can call to You and You will save me (Psalm 107:13). Set me free from all negative emotions that have become a habit. Give me a garment of praise to take away the spirit of heaviness. In Your presence I find fullness of joy.

THANK GOD THAT HE KNOWS AND LOVES YOU

"O LORD, you have searched me and you know me. You know when I sit and when I rise; you perceive my thoughts from afar. You discern my going out and my lying down; you are familiar with all my ways."

PSALM 139:1-3

GOD, I thank You that You know everything about me and You still love me. You know my thoughts and my mistakes, and You still call me Yours. Thank You that You are always with me—teaching and guiding me, comforting and restoring me—and I am never alone. You, Lord, know me better than I know myself. Help me to know You better every day.

The Lord Is Near When We Pray

"The LORD is near to all who call on him, to all who call on him in truth."

PSALM 145:18

LORD, I draw close to You and thank You that You are close to me. I confess the times when I have doubted You were near, because it seemed my prayers went unanswered. Now I know that doubt is in opposition to Your Word. Help me to pray even more fervently during times of unanswered prayer instead of being concerned that nothing will change.

Acknowledge God in Every Area of Your Life

"Trust in the L<small>ORD</small> with all your heart and lean not on your own understanding; in all your ways acknowledge him, and he will make your paths straight."

P<small>ROVERBS</small> 3:5-6

H<small>EAVENLY</small> F<small>ATHER</small>, I ask that You would help me to trust You and Your ways and not depend on my own limited understanding of things. Help me to acknowledge You in every area of my life. If I have shut You out of any part of my life, I ask that You would reveal this to me so I can invite You to reign there. Thank You for making my path straight.

Maintain a Right Heart

"Keep your heart with all diligence, for
out of it spring the issues of life."

PROVERBS 4:23 NKJV

LORD, create in me a clean heart. Set me free from anything that is not of You. Cleanse my heart of all sin, and direct it to Your ways (Psalm 119:36). Help me to hide Your Word in my heart so that I will not sin against You (Psalm 119:11). I don't want any sin in my heart to hinder my prayers to You (Psalm 66:18). Keep me undeceived (Deuteronomy 11:16). Help me not to foolishly trust my own heart, but instead to trust You to reveal the truth I need to see.

THE BENEFITS OF
WAITING ON GOD

*"Blessed is the man who listens to me, watching
daily at my doors, waiting at my doorway."*

PROVERBS 8:34

LORD, I wait on You and listen for Your voice.
Speak to my heart about the things I need to hear.
Teach me all I need to know. Thank You for the
great blessings that await anyone who waits at Your
door and listens for Your voice. In these times of
waiting on You, may the character of Christ be
formed in me and my faith be increased.

Give Yourself Away—
to God and to Others

*"The generous soul will be made rich, and he
who waters will also be watered himself."*

PROVERBS 11:25 NKJV

LORD, teach me how to give to You with a cheerful attitude. Help me to be diligent in this step of obedience. Help me to give to You as You require. Teach my heart to release back to You from all You have given to me. Help me to reject the fear of not having enough. When I become fearful, help me to put my trust in You. You are greater than any lack I may face. Show me specific ways I can give to others. Reveal their needs to me and how I can meet them.

GODLY FEAR

"The fear of the LORD is a fountain of life, to turn one away from the snares of death."

PROVERBS 14:27 NKJV

LORD, Your Word says "though an army may encamp against me, my heart shall not fear" (Psalm 27:3). How grateful I am that when I cry out to You, You hear me and deliver me from all my fears (Psalm 34:4). I know reverence of You brings life and keeps me away from the pitfalls that lead to death. Enable me to have that godly fear in my heart always. Help me to make praise my first reaction to fear whenever it comes upon me. I don't want to deny Your presence by giving place to fear in times of weakness.

GOD HEARS THE PRAYERS OF THE RIGHTEOUS

*"The LORD detests the sacrifice of the wicked,
but the prayer of the upright pleases him."*

PROVERBS 15:8

⟶

DEAR GOD, how grateful I am that You see me as righteous because of my relationship with Jesus. But I know You also want me to choose to *live* righteously as well. I pray my thoughts, words, and actions will be pleasing in Your sight so that my prayers will always be pleasing to Your ears. Enable me to do what's right in every situation.

Good Reasons to Ask God for Wisdom

*"Buy the truth and do not sell it; get
wisdom, discipline and understanding."*

PROVERBS 23:23

LORD, I pray You would give me wisdom so that I
will have a long life of peace, blessing, and happi-
ness. I know with wisdom comes confidence, protection, security, promotion, and guidance. I pray
to have the kind of wisdom that saves me from evil
and enables me to make right decisions. Along with
that, help me to live with understanding, discipline,
revelation, and truth.

WHEN OUR PRAYERS DISPLEASE GOD

*"If anyone turns a deaf ear to the law,
even his prayers are detestable."*

PROVERBS 28:9

ALMIGHTY GOD, help me to know Your laws. Teach me Your Word so that I understand it better every time I read it. Give me insight into Your ways so that they become part of my habits. Speak to my heart whenever my thoughts, words, or actions begin to get off the mark. Keep me on the right path so that my prayers are never detestable to You. Enable me to never grow a deaf ear to Your leading.

TIMING IS EVERYTHING

"He has made everything beautiful in its time. He has also set eternity in the hearts of men; yet they cannot fathom what God has done from beginning to end."

ECCLESIASTES 3:11

LORD, I know Your timing is not the same as mine. I want all the answers to my prayers right now. But You want me to be patient and wait on You. I lay my concerns before You and leave the outcome in Your hands. Help me to rest in the knowledge that Your timing is perfect, just as everything You do is perfect. Thank You that You make all things beautiful—even me and my life—in the appropriate time.

STEP OUT OF DESTRUCTIVE RELATIONSHIPS

*"Two are better than one, because they have
a good reward for their labor. For if they
fall, one will lift up his companion."*

ECCLESIASTES 4:9-10 NKJV

LORD, I thank You for the people You have put into my life. Make all my good relationships stronger. Help me to handle the difficult ones in a way that pleases You. Remove any hopelessly destructive relationship from my life by either changing it for the better or by taking that person out of my life. Give me wisdom about the friends I choose. Help me not to ever be in a relationship with anyone who will lead me off the path You have for me. If there is any relationship I have that is destructive for either of us, enable us both to change in order to make it better or help us to let it go.

A Stream of Refreshing

"You are a garden fountain, a well of flowing water streaming down from Lebanon."

SONG OF SONGS 4:15

LORD, fill me afresh with Your Spirit today and overflow me with Your healing stream so that when I am with anyone else, they will sense Your presence. Make me to be like a well of refreshing water flowing out to others. I know You see me through Your Son, Jesus. I pray others will see Jesus in me, even if they don't fully understand what they are seeing.

STANDING BEFORE OUR HOLY GOD

"'Woe to me!' I cried. 'I am ruined! For I am a man of unclean lips, and I live among a people of unclean lips, and my eyes have seen the King, the LORD Almighty.'"

ISAIAH 6:5

DEAR JESUS, whenever I sense Your holy presence, I am greatly aware of my own unworthiness. And that makes me even more grateful for how much You sacrificed for me, and You did it so that I can come before Your throne with confidence and find mercy and grace in my time of need. Touch me and purify me and help me to separate myself from all that is unholy.

I Will Praise You

"I will praise you, O LORD. Although you were angry with me, your anger has turned away and you have comforted me. Surely God is my salvation; I will trust and not be afraid. The LORD, the LORD is my strength and my song; he has become my salvation."

ISAIAH 12:1-2

LORD, even though I don't always do, say, or think the right thing—and I know sin displeases You—I thank You that You always love me and will hear my confession. Give me the discernment to hide myself in You when I see temptation coming. You are my Savior and my Deliverer, and I lift up praise to You whenever I sense the enemy trying to draw me away from Your path. I praise You in all things.

PEACE FOR YOUR MIND

*"You will keep him in perfect peace, whose mind
is stayed on You, because he trusts in You."*

ISAIAH 26:3 NKJV

LORD, teach me the truth of Your Word so well that
I recognize a lie the moment it presents itself. I know
I cannot move into all You have for me if I believe
lies about myself, my circumstances, or You. Help
me to silence the voice of the enemy by speaking
Your truth. Help me to not entertain thoughts of
unforgiveness against anyone, nor dwell on what has
happened in the past. I pray that Your peace, which
surpasses all understanding, will guard my heart and
mind through Jesus, my Lord (Philippians 4:7).

Knowing Which Way to Go

"Whether you turn to the right or to the left, your ears will hear a voice behind you, saying, 'This is the way; walk in it.'"

Isaiah 30:21

LORD, speak to me about Your will for my life so that I can always walk in it. Your will is a place of safety and protection for me, and I need to know I am headed in the right direction. Help me to hear Your voice speaking to my heart telling me what to do, especially with regard to the decisions I need to make each day of my life.

Praise Is the Purest Form of Prayer

"I provide water in the desert and streams in the wasteland, to give drink to my people, my chosen, the people I formed for myself that they may proclaim my praise."

Isaiah 43:20-21

God, I want to show my love, reverence, devotion, and appreciation for You as I lift You up in worship. I praise You for who You are and for all You have done in this world and in my life. Help me to live every day with praise and thanksgiving in my heart so that I will fulfill my greatest purpose and calling on this earth—which is to worship and glorify You.

Speak Words
That Bring Life

"The Lord GOD has given Me the tongue of
the learned, that I should know how to speak
a word in season to him who is weary."

Isaiah 50:4 NKJV

GOD, help me to speak words that lift up and not
tear down, words that compliment instead of crit-
icize, words that speak unconditional love and not
human expectations, and words that instill confidence and not uneasiness. Where I have said words
that are negative about myself or anyone else, forgive me. I want to be kind with my words and to
daily remember that "the tongue of the wise pro-
motes health" (Proverbs 12:18). Fill me afresh with
Your Holy Spirit and pour into my heart Your love,
peace, and joy. Help me to treat myself and others
with respect, patience, and love.

Speak Good Words
from God's Heart

*"I have put My words in your mouth; I have
covered you with the shadow of My hand."*

Isaiah 51:16 nkjv

Lord, help me refuse to say negative things, even
about myself. Every time I start to say a critical
word, help me to stop immediately and not continue that line of thinking. Teach me to monitor
the words I speak to others. Keep me from saying
wrong words that may hurt someone or diminish
them in any way. Help me not to be careless in this
regard. Teach me to always speak words that are
supported by Your truth and glorify You.

Truly Healed

"Surely He has borne our griefs and carried our sorrows; yet we esteemed Him stricken, smitten by God, and afflicted. But He was wounded for our transgressions, He was bruised for our iniquities; the chastisement for our peace was upon Him, and by His stripes we are healed."

Isaiah 53:4-5 nkjv

Lord, restore health to me and heal me of all my wounds. Enlarge my faith in You and Your name so that I can lay hold of the healing You paid for on the cross. Help me not to give up praying until I see the healing You have for me. I know that when You heal me, I am truly healed (Jeremiah 17:14). Teach me how to pray in power and faith for the healing of others. Every time I pray for someone else, hear my prayer and answer by touching that person with Your healing power. Show me how to pray so that You can do a miracle, not only in my life but also in the lives of other people.

How to Respond to Unanswered Prayer

*"'Sing, O barren woman, you who never bore
a child; burst into song, shout for joy, you
who were never in labor; because more are
the children of the desolate woman than of
her who has a husband,' says the LORD."*

ISAIAH 54:1

LORD, Your Word says to sing praise in the face of unfruitful situations in our lives. So even when my prayers are unanswered I will still praise You, because I know that You can breathe life into any situation—even one that seems dead. When I pray, help me to trust that You have heard my prayers and have not forgotten my request.

THE PROMISES OF GOD

*"'For the mountains shall depart and the hills
be removed, but My kindness shall not depart
from you, nor shall My covenant of peace be
removed,' says the LORD, who has mercy on you."*

ISAIAH 54:10 NKJV

LORD, help me to cling to Your promises so that
they are engraved upon my heart and are alive
within me. Enable me to "not remember the for-
mer things, nor consider the things of old" (Isaiah 43:18). I know You are doing a new thing in
me. I pray You will "make a road in the wilderness
and rivers in the desert" for me (Isaiah 43:18-19). I
know I'm often in a hurry for things to happen, and
I ask You to forgive me when I have tried to put You
on my schedule. Thank You that You "will perfect
that which concerns me" (Psalm 138:8).

PRAYING GOD'S WORD

*"As the rain and the snow come down from heaven,
and do not return to it without watering the earth
and making it bud and flourish...so is my word
that goes out from my mouth: It will not return
to me empty, but will accomplish what I desire
and achieve the purpose for which I sent it."*

ISAIAH 55:10-11

HEAVENLY FATHER, I thank You that Your Word
always accomplishes the purpose for which You
sent it. Enable me to secure the power and life
that is in Your Word by having it planted so firmly
in my heart that it guides everything I do. Help
me to weave Your Word into my prayers so that
it becomes a powerful weapon against which the
enemy cannot prevail.

THE FAST GOD DESIRES

"Is this not the fast that I have chosen: to loose the bonds of wickedness, to undo the heavy burdens, to let the oppressed go free, and that you break every yoke?"

ISAIAH 58:6 NKJV

LORD, reveal ways to pray I don't yet understand as I fast. Help me to do what I can to help others and feed the hungry. Show me where I should extend myself to those who are afflicted or suffering. Help me to honor the Sabbath—Your holy day—by doing what honors You and not going my own way and doing what I want. Help me to want what *You* want. Thank You that as I fast, You will look after the details of my life and give me direction.

TEARING DOWN THE WALL OF SEPARATION

"But your iniquities have separated you from your God; your sins have hidden his face from you, so that he will not hear."

LORD, I know my life does not work when I am not living Your way. Help me to stay undeceived about my own sin so that I can confess it immediately and be cleansed of it. I don't want anything to separate me from You and hinder my prayers by causing You to not hear them. Thank You, Jesus, that You have made a way for me to find forgiveness for my failures.

RECEIVE BEAUTY FOR ASHES

"He has sent me…to bestow on them a crown of beauty instead of ashes, the oil of gladness instead of mourning, and a garment of praise instead of a spirit of despair."

ISAIAH 61:1,3

DEAR GOD, I grieve over my own sins and over any time I have not lived Your way. I don't know how much I must have lost, or the blessings I have forfeited, because of it. But I confess my sins of thought, word, and action to You now and ask that You would give me beauty instead of ashes, gladness instead of mourning, and a garment of praise instead of despair.

Finding Deliverance

*"For Zion's sake I will not keep silent, for
Jerusalem's sake I will not remain quiet, til
her righteousness shines out like the dawn,
her salvation like a blazing torch."*

Isaiah 62:1

Lord, I know my only hope for deliverance and restoration in my life is found in You. You have saved me for eternity and for Your glory, and nothing is impossible with You. I pray You will not give up on me until I am completely set free and restored to total wholeness, and my righteousness shines forth like the morning sun. Thank You for delivering me into the life You have for me.

Praying Without Excuses

*"But the L*ORD *said to me, 'Do not say, "I am only a child." You must go to everyone I send you to and say whatever I command you…' Then the L*ORD *reached out his hand and touched my mouth and said to me, 'Now, I have put my words in your mouth.'"*

JEREMIAH 1:7,9

FATHER GOD, I don't want to make excuses for not doing Your will, but I feel inadequate to do the things You are calling me to do—especially in prayer. Yet I don't want fear to keep me from doing it. I want to depend on You to do it through me. I pray You would put Your words in my mouth so that I can intercede for others by the power of Your Spirit, and I can speak to others the words You give me.

Praying for Your Nation

"This is what the LORD says: 'Stand at the crossroads
and look; ask for the ancient paths, ask where
the good way is, and walk in it, and you will
find rest for your souls. But you said, "We will
not walk in it."…I am bringing disaster on
this people, the fruit of their schemes, because
they have not listened to my words.'"

JEREMIAH 6:16,19

LORD, I come humbly before You and confess the
sins of my nation. Even though there are many
people who believe in You, far too many have
refused to walk Your way. I stand in the gap at the
crossroads and look for the good way and pray for
many more to join me in walking according to Your
law so that disaster will be averted in our land. I
pray that many more people will bow before You
and seek Your ways.

Boasting in God Alone

"This is what the LORD says: 'Let not the wise man boast of his wisdom or the strong man boast of his strength or the rich man boast of his riches, but let him who boasts boast about this: that he understands and knows me, that I am the LORD, who exercises kindness, justice and righteousness on earth, for in these I delight.'"

JEREMIAH 9:23-24

LORD, I confess any pride I have in my heart and I acknowledge it as sin before You. I know that all good things in my life have come from You. Help me to never boast about anything other than the fact that I know You are the Lord. And the only reason I have the potential to do something great is because the greatness of Your Holy Spirit dwells in me, helping me to know You and understand Your ways.

BRING QUESTIONS TO GOD

*"You are always righteous, O LORD, when I bring
a case before you. Yet I would speak with you
about your justice: Why does the way of the wicked
prosper? Why do all the faithless live at ease?"*

JEREMIAH 12:1

GOD, I know You are always good and just, and I
don't question Your ways, but I confess that some-
times I wonder why certain people seem to get away
with murder while others, who are Your servants—
and seem to have done nothing wrong—have so
much suffering in their lives. Help me to see these
things from Your perspective so that I might help
others do the same.

Trust in Your Healer

*"Heal me, O Lord, and I shall be healed; save
me, and I shall be saved, for You are my praise."*

Jeremiah 17:14 NKJV

Lord, thank You for Your healing power on my
behalf. I believe You, Jesus, are the living Word. You
paid the price on the cross to purchase healing for
me. You took my infirmities and bore my sickness.
There is healing in Your name, and I believe You
are my healer. Thank You for Your written Word,
which comes alive in my heart as I read it, speak
it, or hear it. I praise You, Lord, for all Your promises of safety, protection, and healing. I choose to
believe Your Word and have faith in You and Your
power to heal.

ASK GOD FOR DISCERNMENT

"This is what the LORD Almighty says: 'Do not listen to what the prophets are prophesying to you; they fill you with false hopes. They speak visions from their own minds, not from the mouth of the LORD.'"

JEREMIAH 23:16

GOD, help me to hear Your voice speaking to my heart. Give me discernment so I can always distinguish between those who speak Your truth and those who give false prophecies filled either with fear or false hope. Help me to examine what I hear against the teaching of Your Word. Holy Spirit, guide me in all truth just as You have promised. Help me to identify what is from You and what is not.

GOD'S PLANS
STILL REQUIRE PRAYER
ON OUR PART

*"'For I know the plans I have for you,' declares
the LORD, 'plans to prosper you and not to harm
you, plans to give you hope and a future.'"*

JEREMIAH 29:11

LORD, I thank You that Your plans for me are for
good—to prosper me and give me a future and a
hope. Help me to obey You in every area of my life
so that I don't do anything that would thwart Your
plans for my future. I seek You about my future now
and ask You to help me to hear Your voice leading
me every step of the way. Give me a vision for the
future that brings peace to my heart about it.

Learning to Listen

"Therefore, this is what the Lord God Almighty, the God of Israel, says: 'Listen!'"

Jeremiah 35:17

Almighty God, help me to be a good listener to Your voice speaking to my heart. I don't want to drown it out with the noise and busyness of life. Help me to take every thought captive in obedience to Your Word. Keep me from entertaining unrighteousness in my thought life. Enable me to be diligent in not allowing anything into my mind that does not glorify You.

Paying Attention to God's Direction

"Zedekiah son of Josiah was made king of Judah by Nebuchadnezzar king of Babylon; he reigned in place of Jehoiachin son of Jehoiakim. Neither he nor his attendants nor the people of the land paid any attention to the words the LORD had spoken through Jeremiah the prophet."

JEREMIAH 37:1-2

FATHER GOD, I ask You for clear direction in my life. Help me to hear and understand what it is. I don't want to miss Your instructions to my heart because I wouldn't listen. Help me to act immediately on the guidance You give me and not ignore it. Show me what to do and enable me to do it. Enable me to pay attention to Your every word and direction to me.

Knowing What to Do

"Pray that the LORD your God will tell us where we should go and what we should do."

Jeremiah 42:3

LORD GOD, I pray You would show me where to go and what to do. I want to always be in the right place at the right time. I lift up to You the specific decisions I need to make today with regard to certain situations in my life. Enable me to hear Your voice instructing me, and help me to do what You are showing me to do. I cannot move forward unless I know You are guiding me.

GOD WILL GET
YOU THROUGH

"'I will surely deliver you,
and you shall not fall by the sword;
but your life shall be as a prize to you,
because you have put your trust
in Me,' says the LORD."

JEREMIAH 39:18 NKJV

LORD, I pray You will be with me in the most difficult and trying areas of my life, helping me in ways I may not even be able to comprehend. I know that even though there may be troubles ahead, when I walk with You, You won't let me fall. When I go through difficult situations, I won't complain, for I know You will make a way through or a means of escape.

Finding Hope in the Midst of Sorrow

"Arise, cry out in the night, as the watches of the night begin; pour out your heart like water in the presence of the LORD. Lift up your hands to him."

LAMENTATIONS 2:19

LORD, I pour out my heart before You regarding the things in my life that cause me grief. I lift my hands to You because I know You are my hope and Your compassion for me never fails. Heal me of all emotional pain, and use the sorrow I have suffered for good. I pray that in Your presence I will find comfort and restoration. I cry out to You regarding all I care about.

FINDING A NEW HEART

*"I will give them an undivided heart and put a
new spirit in them; I will remove from them their
heart of stone and give them a heart of flesh."*

EZEKIEL 11:19

DEAR GOD, I pray You will fill me with Your love,
and help me to keep my heart from wandering away
from You. Make my heart to be undivided and take
away any hard-heartedness in me. I invite You to
take charge of my mind and soul. Help me to give
complete control to You. Light a flame of desire in
me for You that never grows dim or goes out.

The Promise
of a Fresh Start

"Rid yourselves of all the offenses you have committed, and get a new heart and a new spirit. Why will you die, O house of Israel?"

EZEKIEL 18:31

LORD, I pray You would take away everything in my heart that is not right before You. Help me to be rid of bad attitudes and wrong thinking. Show me anything that has taken root in my heart that should not be there so that I can free myself of it before there is a serious price to pay. Help me clear the slate and begin again with a new heart and spirit.

GETTING FREE OF
THE BURDEN OF SIN

*"There you will remember your conduct
and all the actions by which you have
defiled yourselves, and you will loathe
yourselves for all the evil you have done."*

EZEKIEL 20:43

LORD, I don't want to look back over my life—even
as recently as yesterday—and feel bad about myself
because of the things I have done wrong. Help me
to quickly recognize and confess sin. Enable me
to live in such a way that I don't have regret over
my words, thoughts, or actions. Help me to fully
repent so that You will fully lift the burden of sin
from me.

STANDING IN THE GAP FOR OUR NATION

"I looked for a man among them who would build up the wall and stand before me in the gap on behalf of the land so I would not have to destroy it, but I found none."

EZEKIEL 22:30

ALMIGHTY GOD, I lift up my nation to You, with all its sin and rebellion, and ask that You would have mercy upon us and help us not to reap the full consequences of what we have sown. I stand in the gap to invoke Your power on our behalf. Do not judge us as we deserve, but rather pour out Your Spirit over this land and bring millions of people to You.

MOVING IN THE SPIRIT

"And I will put my Spirit in you and move you to follow my decrees and be careful to keep my laws."

EZEKIEL 36:27

LORD, lead me by the power of Your Holy Spirit so that I will always obey Your Word and follow Your laws. Give me the discipline I need to do what I must do. Thank You that You have put Your Holy Spirit within me to guide me in all things. Help me to follow Your leading and not run ahead or behind chasing after my own ways. I seek after only You.

Bringing Dead Things to Life

"This is what the Sovereign LORD says to these bones: I will make breath enter you, and you will come to life."

Ezekiel 37:5

DEAR GOD, there are areas of my life that seem dead to me; they need a new infusion of *Your* life. There are dreams I have had that seem as if they have died because for so long they have not yet been realized. I know if You can make dry bones into a vast army, You can bring life to anything worth praying about. Breathe new life into my mind, soul, and body today.

SEEING GOD IN THE DARK

"During the night the mystery was revealed to Daniel in a vision. Then Daniel praised the God of heaven and said: 'Praise be to the name of God for ever and ever; wisdom and power are his.'"

DANIEL 2:19-20

LORD, it seems that in the middle of the night all problems appear larger. At those times I am reminded that You never sleep, and I can come to You and cling to Your presence. I pray that at those times You will give me the treasures of darkness, stored in secret places, as You have spoken of in Your Word. I pray You will fill my darkness with Your light and give me rest. Give me the revelation I need for the situation I face.

CRYING OUT
FOR GOD'S MERCY

"Now, our God, hear the prayers and petitions of your servant… We do not make requests of you because we are righteous, but because of your great mercy."

DANIEL 9:17-18

DEAR GOD, I come to You, not because I am worthy, but because *You* are. You are full of mercy, and I need Your mercy extended to me today. I need help with all things, but especially with certain situations in my life right now. I thank You that Your help isn't dependent upon *my* good works, but upon who *You* are—the God of mercy and grace.

FINDING FAITH TO
WAIT FOR THE ANSWER

"Then he continued, 'Do not be afraid, Daniel.
Since the first day that you set your mind to gain
understanding and to humble yourself before
your God, your words were heard, and I have
come in response to them. But the prince of the
Persian kingdom resisted me twenty-one days.'"

DANIEL 10:12-13

HEAVENLY FATHER, help me to wait patiently for the answers to my prayers. Increase my faith to know that when I pray, You hear the cries of my heart and will answer in Your perfect timing and Your perfect way. Help me to continue to pray and not give up, no matter how long it takes or how many obstacles the enemy throws in my path.

Finding God's Forgiveness and Love

"Take words with you and return to the LORD. Say to him: 'Forgive all our sins and receive us graciously, that we may offer the fruit of our lips.'"

Hosea 14:2

Dear God, I recognize how sinful and needy I am. I know I cannot save myself in any way, but You have saved me in every way. That's why I humble myself before You, first of all in confession of my sins. Secondly, I praise You for all You have done for me by extending Your forgiveness, love, and mercy my way. I love You above all else.

It's Never Too Late to Turn to God

"I will repay you for the years the locusts have eaten—the great locust and the young locust, the other locusts and the locust swarm—my great army that I sent among you."

JOEL 2:25

DEAR GOD, I thank You that it is never too late to turn to You and see restoration happen. Even though I may feel there has been time wasted in my life when I didn't live fully for You, I pray You would redeem the time and help me to make up for it. Restore anything that has been lost, wasted, or ruined so I can give You the glory.

Pray for Godly Friends

*"Do two walk together unless they
have agreed to do so?"*

Amos 3:3

Lord, I pray I would always have good godly friends, and that we would influence, encourage, and inspire each other to walk closer to You. I pray for friends who will tell me the truth in love, give me sound counsel, and be a help in times of trouble. Enable me to be that kind of friend too. Help me to live in unity with the people You put in my life as godly friends.

Delivering God's Message

*"The LORD said, 'You have had pity on the plant
for which you have not labored...
should I not pity Nineveh, that great city?'"*

JONAH 4:10-11 NKJV

LORD, I know there are people in the city around me who need to hear Your message of hope and truth—people whom I might not even notice, but whom You love deeply. Reveal them to me so I can pray for them and perhaps speak a good word from You to certain people. Prepare their hearts to receive from me and most of all from You.

Rising Up Out
of the Darkness

"Do not gloat over me, my enemy! Though
I have fallen, I will rise. Though I sit in
darkness, the Lord will be my light."

Micah 7:8

Thank You, Lord, that even if I were to fall off
the path You have for me to walk, You will always
be there to lift me up and back on it again when I
repent of my sins. I thank You that even if I sink
into darkness, You will be my light. I praise You
as the light of my life and keeper of the flame that
burns in my heart for eternity. The enemy will never
have victory over me because You are my God.

KEEP PRAYING
NO MATTER WHAT

"How long, O LORD, must I call for help, but you do not listen? Or cry out to you, 'Violence!' but you do not save?"

HABAKKUK 1:2

LORD, help me to have the understanding and faith I need to keep praying and not give up if my prayers are not answered right away. I know Your ways are perfect. Help me to not become discouraged in the time of waiting for Your help, but rather to continue praying until I see Your will done in all the things You put on my heart to pray about.

THANK GOD
FOR HIS LOVE

*"The LORD your God is with you, he is
mighty to save. He will take great delight
in you, he will quiet you with his love, he
will rejoice over you with singing."*

ZEPHANIAH 3:17

LORD, I have great joy in knowing You are always
with me and have the power to save me from the
plans of the enemy. Help me to remember at all
times—even when I go through difficult situations
that shake the very foundation of my soul—that
my foundation is in You and my security is sus-
tained by Your great love for me.

DON'T NEGLECT
YOUR WALK WITH GOD

"'You expected much, but see, it turned out to be little. What you brought home, I blew away. Why?' declares the LORD Almighty. 'Because of my house, which remains a ruin, while each of you is busy with his own house.'"

HAGGAI 1:9

GOD, help me to not be concerned with outward appearances, selfish pursuits, and the condition of my own house, but rather to be concerned with spiritual growth, unselfish service, and the condition of *Your* house. I want to always have my priorities in order so that my walk with You continues to grow closer and deeper. I don't want my own selfishness to stand in the way of Your blessings.

By His Spirit

"So he said to me, 'This is the word of the LORD to Zerubbabel: "Not by might nor by power, but by my Spirit," says the Lord Almighty.'"

ZECHARIAH 4:6

ALMIGHTY GOD, I acknowledge I cannot do all You have called me to do, except that Your Spirit enables me to do it. I depend on You to help me get where I need to go. I worship You as the light of my life who illuminates my path and guides my every step. I praise You as the all-powerful God of the universe for whom nothing is too hard.

DEVELOPING A HEART FOR WORSHIP

"Ask all the people of the land and the priests, 'When you fasted and mourned in the fifth and seventh months for the past seventy years, was it really for me that you fasted?'"

ZECHARIAH 7:5

DEAR LORD, help me to never get to the point where I take Your presence in my life lightly. Help me not to allow the things I do for You to become routine so that they lose their life and meaning in my heart. I know my fasting, praying, and worshipping mean nothing to You if they mean nothing to me. Help me to do all things in a way that pleases You.

Praying for Healing

*"But to you who fear My name the
Sun of Righteousness shall arise
with healing in His wings."*

Malachi 4:2 nkjv

Dear Lord, how grateful I am that You came as our Healer. Thank You for mercifully understanding how much we need Your healing hand. I ask for Your healing touch upon my body today and whenever I need it. I know when You heal me, I will be healed completely. At the same time I ask for Your guidance and wisdom in knowing how to properly take care of my body.

Make My Heart Pure

*"Blessed are the pure in heart, for
they shall see God."*

Matthew 5:8 nkjv

Holy Spirit, align my heart with Yours. Flush
out of my heart all that is dark and wrong and
replace it with more of You. Search my heart and
make changes wherever they are needed. Soften my
heart where it has become hard. Purify my heart
where it has become polluted. Help me to set nothing wicked before my eyes. Lord, I pray that You
would take away anything in my heart that keeps
me from being a full partaker of Your holiness
(Hebrews 12:10). Help me to praise You with my
whole heart.

Praying for Someone You Don't Think Deserves It

"I say to you, love your enemies, bless those who curse you, do good to those who hate you, and pray for those who spitefully use you and persecute you."

Matthew 5:44 NKJV

LORD, help me to obey Your commandment to love my enemies and to pray for those who persecute me. I know you have heard and answered the prayers of others for *me* when I didn't deserve it; help me to do the same for them. Give me Your heart of love so that I can pray for people who hurt or disappoint me.

Jesus Teaches Us How to Pray

"This, then, is how you should pray: 'Our Father in heaven, hallowed be your name, your kingdom come, your will be done on earth as it is in heaven. Give us today our daily bread. Forgive us our debts, as we also have forgiven our debtors. And lead us not into temptation, but deliver us from the evil one.'"

Matthew 6:9-13

Heavenly Father, I praise Your holy name. I pray You will reign in my life and rule in this world. Pour out Your Spirit upon me so that Your will is done. Forgive me of all my sins; help me forgive others. I depend on Your provision, forgiveness, and protection from the enemy. I praise You for all You are and all You do.

Fast and Pray to Win

"When you fast, anoint your head and wash
your face, so that you do not appear to men
to be fasting, but to your Father who is
in the secret place; and your Father who
sees in secret will reward you openly."

Matthew 6:17-18 nkjv

Lord, help me to fast and pray to Your glory. Enable me to put aside one of my favorite activities—eating the food You have provided for me—in favor of exalting You as everything in my life. Show me how often and how long I should fast, and enable me to accomplish it. Help me to be well enough and strong enough to fast in the way You want me to. Thank You that when I fast, You will break down the strongholds of the enemy in my life and loose all bonds of wickedness. I pray You will break any wrong thinking in me and release me from the burdens I have been carrying.

Ask, Seek, and Knock

"Ask and it will be given to you; seek and you will find; knock and the door will be opened to you. For everyone who asks receives; he who seeks finds; and to him who knocks, the door will be opened."

Matthew 7:7-8

Lord, I come to You in faith, believing that You reward those who diligently seek You. Your Word says You desire to give good gifts to those who ask for them. I ask that the desires of my heart be aligned with Your will so that they will come to pass. I knock on the door of opportunity for my life, and anticipate it being opened by You.

The Value of Time Alone with God

*"After he had dismissed them, he went up on
a mountainside by himself to pray. When
evening came, he was there alone."*

Matthew 14:23

Dear Lord, help me to find the time I need every day to be alone with You. Escaping all the diversions and busyness seems to be a constant struggle, and I need a greater ability to shut out everything and find solitude with You in prayer. Help me to daily secure a place of peace and quiet so that I can hear Your voice speaking to my heart.

CREATING A
SYMPHONY OF PRAYER

*"Again, I tell you that if two of you on earth
agree about anything you ask for, it will be
done for you by my Father in heaven."*

MATTHEW 18:19

LORD, help me to find believers with whom I can
agree in prayer on a regular basis. I pray we will be
in agreement about the truth of Your Word and the
power of Your Holy Spirit. You have said that one
can put a thousand to flight and two can put ten
thousand to flight. I pray for enough prayer partners to put all of the enemy's forces attacking our
lives to flight.

PRAY AS THOUGH
YOUR LIFE DEPENDS ON IT

*"Whatever things you ask in prayer,
believing, you will receive."*

MATTHEW 21:22 NKJV

LORD, teach me to pray. Help me to pray about not just *my* needs, but also the needs of others. Show me how to pray about everything. Help me to leave the things I pray about at Your feet and in Your hands. Teach me to trust You so much that I don't have preconceived ideas about the way my prayers must be answered. I know it is my job to pray and Your job to answer. Help me to do my job and let You do Yours. Help me to trust that You will answer in Your way and in Your time.

WANTING GOD'S WILL

"Going a little farther, he fell with his face to the ground and prayed, 'My Father, if it is possible, may this cup be taken from me. Yet not as I will, but as you will.'"

MATTHEW 26:39

HEAVENLY FATHER, more than anything I want Your will to be done in my life. Even though I want You to take away all my pain and suffering, more than that I want all of Your blessings. Even though I want things to turn out the way I want them to, above all I want Your will to be done and not my own. Reveal Your will to me and help me to pray accordingly.

Going Directly to God

"And Jesus cried out again with a loud voice, and yielded up His Spirit. Then behold, the veil of the temple was torn in two from top to bottom."

Matthew 27:50-51 nkjv

Thank You, Jesus, that because You gave Your life in sacrifice for mine, the veil of separation has been torn in two and in Your name I can go directly to God in intercession. Thank You, Lord, that I can come to You with my prayers. Help me to remember that I can always confidently come to Your throne feeling assured that I will receive Your grace and mercy to help me in my times of need.

The Power to
Fight Temptation

*"He was in the desert forty days, being
tempted by Satan. He was with the wild
animals, and angels attended him."*

MARK 1:13

LORD, equip me to resist all temptation from the
enemy. Enable me to be so prepared before temptation happens that I recognize the enemy's tac-
tics from the moment they manifest. Teach me to
rebuke the enemy by having a great knowledge of
Your Word. Enable me to resist entertaining temptation for even a moment and to turn to You immediately so that I can stand strong.

Finding Freedom from What Keeps You Bound

*"He replied, 'This kind can come
out only by prayer.'"*

Mark 9:29

Lord, I see in Your Word that prayer is the key to being set free, and prayer together with fasting together is even more powerful. I pray You will help me to understand the authority You have given me in prayer to release Your power from heaven in order to see freedom happen in my life and in the lives of those for whom I pray. Help me to fast and pray—if only a day—to release from my life the things that shouldn't be there.

NOTHING IS
IMPOSSIBLE WITH GOD

"Jesus looked at them and said, 'With man this is impossible, but not with God; all things are possible with God.'"

MARK 10:27

GOD, You are all-powerful and nothing is too hard for You, not even changing the most difficult circumstances of my life. What is impossible for me is not impossible for You, so I ask that You would do the impossible and transform me into a holy person full of Your love, peace, and joy. Make right the things that are wrong. Enable me to do great things by the power of Your Spirit.

THE POWER
OF FORGIVENESS

"And when you stand praying, if you hold anything
against anyone, forgive him, so that your
Father in heaven may forgive you your sins."

MARK 11:25

LORD, I pray You would reveal any place in my
heart where I have not forgiven someone. I know
I have asked this before, but I also know how easy
it is to let resentment build up, even though I try
not to allow that to happen. I don't want to close
off the forgiveness You have for me because I have
not forgiven someone else. I want to please You by
not holding anything against anyone.

THE COST
OF FORGIVENESS

"So when the centurion, who stood opposite Him,
saw that He cried out like this and breathed His
last, he said, 'Truly this Man was the Son of God.'"

MARK 15:39 NKJV

DEAR LORD, help me to never forget the great price
You paid so that I could be forgiven. I don't want
to ever take for granted the sacrifice You made on
my behalf so that no further sacrifice of life needs
to be made. Now the sacrifice I must make is one
of thanksgiving and praise to You for all that You
have done to set me free from the consequences of
my own sin.

Be Holy as
God Is Holy

*"We, being delivered from the hand of our enemies,
might serve Him without fear, in holiness and
righteousness before Him all the days of our life."*

LUKE 1:74-75 NKJV

LORD, help me to be holy as You are holy. Jesus, help me to walk as You walked on earth. Enable me to be an imitator of You (Ephesians 5:1). Wash over me with Your holiness and cleanse me from the inside out of anything in me that is not holy. Reveal whatever is hidden within me that I need to be rid of—any attitudes, thoughts, or sin that must be gone from my life. Separate me from all that separates me from You, Lord. Give me the conviction and strength I need to step away from whatever is not compatible with Your holiness in me.

FORGIVE AND YOU WILL BE FORGIVEN

"Judge not, and you shall not be judged.
Condemn not, and you shall not be condemned.
Forgive, and you will be forgiven."

LUKE 6:37 NKJV

LORD, show me any way I need to ask someone to forgive me so that we both can be healed and set free. Lord, take away anything of anger, bitterness, or resentment in my heart. Pour out Your Spirit upon me and cleanse me of all that is not of You. Enable me to be a person who lives in the forgiveness You have given me so I can extend forgiveness freely toward others (Ephesians 4:32).

Our God-Given Authority

*"I have given you authority to trample on snakes
and scorpions and to overcome all the power
of the enemy; nothing will harm you."*

LUKE 10:19

DEAR GOD, help me to fully understand the authority You have given me over the enemy of my soul. Thank You, Jesus, that because of what You accomplished on the cross, the enemy is defeated. Enable me to always recognize his lies and deception and be able to stand strong on the truth of Your Word so that I can control his access to my life. Thank You for Your protection over me.

Why Prayer Works

*"I tell you, though he will not get up and give
him the bread because he is his friend, yet
because of the man's boldness he will get
up and give him as much as he needs."*

Luke 11:8

LORD, help me to be bold and persistent in prayer.
I don't want to be arrogant or presumptuous, as if
You owe me anything, but rather to be confident
in what Jesus accomplished on the cross that took
away Satan's rule and established Your own. Help
me to have great faith that prayer works so that I am
confident enough to ask for great things, knowing
that You will answer in a great way.

LET TIME WITH GOD TAKE THE PLACE OF WORRYING

*"Who of you by worrying can add
a single hour to his life?"*

LUKE 12:25

DEAR GOD, I pray You would help me to stop worrying about things and start spending more time in Your presence. I know the time I waste by worrying is better used to pray and to hear Your voice speaking to my heart. You are my source of strength, hope, love, peace, and rest, and I want to be connected with You and not the things that worry me.

SEEK GOD'S KINGDOM

"Do not fear, little flock, for it is your Father's good pleasure to give you the kingdom."

LUKE 12:32 NKJV

LORD, I come humbly before You and seek Your kingdom and Your dominion in my heart and life above all else. May Your kingdom be established wherever I go and in whatever I do. Make me a pure vessel for Your power to go forth and proclaim the rule of King Jesus wherever You have given me influence and opportunity to do so.

THE HIDDEN
POWER OF PRAISE

*"One of them, when he saw he was healed,
came back, praising God in a loud voice."*

LUKE 17:15

HEAVENLY FATHER, I thank You for all of the many blessings You have bestowed upon my life. I praise You especially as my healer and thank You for all the times You have healed me in the past and will heal me in the future. Thank You that even as I praise You now, Your healing presence is penetrating my life and making me whole. Touch me with Your healing power today.

Pray That Your Faith Will Not Fail

"But I have prayed for you, Simon, that your faith may not fail. And when you have turned back, strengthen your brothers."

Luke 22:32

Father God, I pray my faith will not fail when I am put to the test. Help me to resist doubt and fear so that my foundation will be built solidly in Christ and therefore will not crumble. Enable me to be a person who strengthens the faith of others because my faith in You is so great. Help me to stand strong no matter what is happening.

FATHER, I FORGIVE THEM

"Jesus said, 'Father, forgive them, for they do not know what they are doing.' And they divided up his clothes by casting lots."

LUKE 23:34

LORD, I pray You would help me to forgive others the way You do. You willingly forgave the unforgivable. I know I can't forgive the unthinkable without You enabling me to do so. Help me to take my focus off whether people deserve to be forgiven or not and instead focus on becoming more like You. You are the only One who knows the whole story.

Know Who Your Father Is

"As many as received Him, to them He gave the right to become children of God, to those who believe in His name."

John 1:12 NKJV

Heavenly Father, I thank You that You have given me the right to become Your child (John 1:12). Help me to live in Your love and comprehend the depth of Your care and concern for me. Take away any barrier that keeps me from fully understanding what it means to trust You as my heavenly Father. Help me to take on a family resemblance so that I have Your eyes, Your heart, and Your mind.

RESPONDING
to GOD's LOVE

*"For God so loved the world that he gave his
one and only Son, that whoever believes in
him shall not perish but have eternal life."*

JOHN 3:16

LORD JESUS, it is hard to comprehend love so great
as Yours. You laid down Your life for me so that I
can live forever with You. I ask You to help me to lay
down my life fully for You in serving Your purpose
here on earth. My response to Your first loving me
is to love You wholeheartedly in return. Forgive me
on the days I fail to show my love to You.

True Worship

*"The hour is coming, and now is, when
the true worshipers will worship the
Father in spirit and truth; for the Father
is seeking such to worship Him."*

JOHN 4:23 NKJV

LORD, it is my greatest privilege to exalt You above all and proclaim that You are King of kings and Lord of lords. I praise You for Your Holy Spirit, who leads and comforts me. I praise You for Your wisdom and revelation. I praise You for Your peace and joy. Thank You that You are in charge of my life and nothing is too hard for You. Thank You for enabling me to do what I could never do without You. Lord, help me to worship You in ways that are pleasing in Your sight.

God Always Hears You When You Pray

"Jesus looked up and said, 'Father, I thank you that you have heard me. I knew that you always hear me, but I said this for the benefit of the people standing here, that they may believe that you sent me.'"

JOHN 11:41-42

FATHER GOD, I thank You that I am Your child and a joint heir with Christ. Because of that, I can trust that You always hear my prayers. Help me to maintain ongoing communication with You, just as Jesus did, so that I may have a deep and abiding walk with You and You will be glorified because of it. Thank You for caring about the cares of my heart.

Welcome the Holy Spirit's Presence

"I will pray the Father, and He will give you another Helper, that He may abide with you forever—the Spirit of truth, whom the world cannot receive, because it neither sees Him nor knows Him; but you know Him, for He dwells with you and will be in you."

John 14:16-17 NKJV

Lord, teach me everything I need to know about You. Enable me to exhibit faithfulness, gentleness, and self-control (Galatians 5:22-23). You are the Spirit of wisdom, grace, holiness, and life. You are the Spirit of counsel, might, and knowledge (Isaiah 11:2). Spirit of truth, help me to know the truth in all things. Thank You for leading and guiding me. Thank You for being my Helper and Comforter. Thank You that Your Spirit within me enables me to walk in Your ways and do Your commands (Ezekiel 36:27).

HAVING PEACE
ABOUT YOUR FUTURE

*"Peace I leave with you, My peace I give to
you; not as the world gives do I give to you."*

JOHN 14:27

DEAR GOD, the only reason I have peace about the
future is because my future is found in You. Even
though I don't know the details about what is to
come, I know that You know everything, and my
future is in Your hands. Help me to walk faithfully
with You every day—in prayer and Your Word—
so that I can move into the purposes You have for
my life.

Remaining in Him

"If you remain in me and my words remain in you,
ask whatever you wish, and it will be given you."

John 15:7

Lord, help me to walk close to You every day and stay constantly in communication with You—both by talking and listening to You speak to my heart. Help me to stay deeply in Your Word, learning more about You and getting to know You better. Help me to increase in the knowledge of Your ways and Your will.

GOD SEES OUR
HEART TOWARD HIM

*"The Father Himself loves you, because
you have loved Me, and have believed
that I came forth from God."*

JOHN 16:27 NKJV

DEAR GOD, I pray I would have a heart of love for You and Your ways that is always pleasing in Your sight. I don't want to be a person who shows love for You with only words. I want to show it with my actions, my obedience to Your laws, and the way I live my life. Thank You that You love me at all times—even when I don't do everything right.

Jesus' Prayer for You

"My prayer is not for them alone. I pray also for those who will believe in me through their message, that all of them may be one, Father, just as you are in me and I am in you."

John 17:20-21

LORD JESUS, just as You prayed for me to be one with You and one with others, I pray You would help me to do that. Enable me to always be in unity with other believers, no matter what church, race, culture, denomination, city, state, or country they are from. Use this unity I have with You and with others to draw unbelievers to You. Use it to help us pray together in power.

BELIEVING
WITHOUT SEEING

"Then Jesus told him, 'Because you have seen me, you have believed; blessed are those who have not seen and yet have believed.'"

JOHN 20:29

LORD, I know You want to bless me in countless ways that require believing without seeing. Help me to have the kind of strong faith I need in order to overcome all doubt. Help me to have faith in Your Word and Your promises, and in Your love, goodness, and power. Help me to trust that You are answering my prayers even when I can't see it.

Staying Devoted to Prayer

*"They devoted themselves to the apostles'
teaching and to the fellowship, to the
breaking of bread and to prayer."*

Acts 2:42

Dear God, help me to be diligent to study Your Word. Teach me from it so that I can understand it perfectly. Help me to be in communion with other believers so we can be frequently in prayer together. Enable me to maintain that direct line to You by praying constantly and devotedly as You bring things to my mind that need to be covered in prayer.

Praying for Spiritual Leaders and Servants

"They presented these men to the apostles, who prayed and laid their hands on them."

Acts 6:6

GOD, I ask You to bless all those in full-time ministry. I pray first of all for my pastor, that You would bless him and his family in every way. I pray for all other pastors and staff members at my church to be blessed by You and led by Your Spirit. Keep them all safe and protect them from any attacks of the enemy. Help them to stand strong against every temptation.

Seeing in the Dark

*"The Lord told him, 'Go to the house of Judas
on Straight Street and ask for a man from
Tarsus named Saul, for he is praying.'"*

Acts 9:11

LORD, just as You appeared to Saul and blinded
him in order to get his attention and do a miraculous turnaround in his life, I know You have some-
times allowed me to get to a dark place in my own
life where I cannot see without Your help. At those
times, help me to do as Saul did and pray fervently,
so that my spiritual sight can be restored and Your
will be done.

Changing the World with Our Prayers

"While they were worshiping the Lord and fasting, the Holy Spirit said, 'Set apart for me Barnabas and Saul for the work to which I have called them.'"

Acts 13:2

Lord, I know my calling and purpose is revealed in prayer. I know it is defined within a church body of believers with whom I can grow. Help me to be in the church body You want me to be in so that I can pray with others in unity and power and be refined by Your Spirit. Enable me to be set apart for the work You have for me to do.

FASTING WHEN I FACE DIFFICULT DECISIONS

"Paul and Barnabas appointed elders for them in each church and, with prayer and fasting, committed them to the Lord, in whom they had put their trust."

ACTS 14:23

LORD GOD, I know when I fast and pray my prayers gain new power. Help me to do that whenever I have to make important decisions and I must have Your guidance. Help me to have the discipline to fast regularly so that I can be prepared when I have to make quick decisions. Make me ready to handle the great opportunities You have ahead for me.

A Parting Prayer

"But when our time was up, we left and continued
on our way. All the disciples and their wives
and children accompanied us out of the city,
and there on the beach we knelt to pray."

ACTS 21:5

DEAR GOD, help me to remember when I am with people who are about to leave on a journey—no matter how long or short—that I need to pray for them to have safety and guidance. Help me to not forget to pray for my own family members who are leaving home to start their day, or any guests in my house who are leaving to be about their business or to travel home.

GOD NEVER DISAPPOINTS

"Hope does not disappoint, because the love
of God has been poured out in our hearts
by the Holy Spirit who was given to us."

ROMANS 5:5 NKJV

LORD, when I pray for a person or a situation and don't see changes, help me to not put my hope in answered prayer, but rather to put my hope in You, the One who *answers* my prayers. Where I have put my hope and expectations on people or circumstances, I confess that as a lack of faith in You and Your Word. I take comfort in Your Word and Your promises. I trust in You—the God of hope—who has given me every reason to hope. In Your presence is where my heart has found a home.

RECEIVE ALL JESUS
DIED FOR YOU TO HAVE

*"If Christ is in you, the body is dead because of sin,
but the Spirit is life because of righteousness."*

ROMANS 8:10 NKJV

LORD, thank You that I have the Holy Spirit within me and am no longer controlled by my flesh. Thank You that I have access to a life of hope, healing, power, love, freedom, fulfillment, and purpose. Help me to understand all that You accomplished on the cross. Enable me to live like the new creation You have made me to be. Help me to see my life from Your perspective. Teach me how to receive all that You died to give me.

WELCOME THE HOLY SPIRIT'S PRESENCE

"As many as are led by the Spirit of God, these are sons of God. For you did not receive the spirit of bondage again to fear, but you received the Spirit of adoption by whom we cry out, 'Abba, Father.' The Spirit Himself bears witness with our spirit that we are children of God."

ROMANS 8:14-16 NKJV

LORD, in Your presence everything makes sense. When I am with You, I feel Your peace, love, and joy rise in me. When I have not spent enough time with You, I greatly miss that priceless sense of the fullness of Your presence. I come before You and ask You to fill me afresh with Your Holy Spirit today. Cleanse me with Your living water. Wash away anything in my heart of doubt, fear, or worry. Take away everything in me that is not of You. Do a complete work in me so that I can show Your pure love to others.

WHEN WORDS DON'T COME

"In the same way, the Spirit helps us in our weakness. We do not know what we ought to pray for, but the Spirit himself intercedes for us with groans that words cannot express. And he who searches our hearts knows the mind of the Spirit, because the Spirit intercedes for the saints in accordance with God's will."

ROMANS 8:26-27

LORD, I don't know how to pray about certain things, but *You* do. Holy Spirit, help me in my weakness by interceding *for* me and *through* me. You know the will of the Father and You know what to pray. Guide me and teach me, especially when I have exhausted all words. Help me to communicate my deepest thoughts, feelings, fears, and doubts, so that my prayers are pleasing to You.

RECOGNIZE YOUR PURPOSE AND WORK TO FULFILL IT

"We know that all things work together for good to those who love God, to those who are the called according to His purpose."

ROMANS 8:28 NKJV

LORD, You knew me before I was born. Thank You that You predestined me to be saved and conformed to the image of Jesus. Give me a clear sense of Your purpose in my life. May everything I do support Your plans for my life. Show me the gifts You have put in me and how I can best develop them and use them for Your pleasure. Help me to live every day with a deep sense of Your purpose in my life.

Nothing Can Separate Me from Your Love

"I am persuaded that neither death nor life,
nor angels nor principalities nor powers, nor
things present nor things to come, nor height
nor depth, nor any other created thing, shall
be able to separate us from the love of God
which is in Christ Jesus our Lord."

Romans 8:38-39 NKJV

Lord, fill my heart with Your love in greater measure so I can be the whole person You created me to be. Give me Your heart of love for others. I pray I will be so filled with Your love that it overflows to other people in a way they can perceive it. Show me the loving thing to do in every situation. How grateful I am that nothing can separate me from Your love, no matter where I go or what I do—not even my own failings (Romans 8:35-39). Thank You, Lord, that Your unfailing love and mercy surround me because I trust in You.

PLEASING GOD IN CARING FOR YOUR BODY

*"Therefore, I urge you, brothers, in view of
God's mercy, to offer your bodies as living
sacrifices, holy and pleasing to God—
this is your spiritual act of worship."*

ROMANS 12:1

LORD, help me to rest at night, as You created me
to do. Help me to exercise as I should so that my
body stays cleansed, active, and strong. Where I
have long-entrenched bad habits when it comes to
proper care for my body, I ask You to reveal them
all to me and enable me to take the necessary steps
to get free. Help me to love and appreciate my body
and not be critical of it. Enable me to choose life
(Deuteronomy 30:19). Even though my flesh and
heart may fail, You are the strength of my heart forever (Psalm 73:26).

Take Control of Your Thoughts

"Do not be conformed to this world, but be transformed by the renewing of your mind, that you may prove what is that good and acceptable and perfect will of God."

Romans 12:2 NKJV

Lord, help me to cast down every thought I have that is not glorifying to You. Enable me to bring my thoughts into captivity and obedience to You and Your ways. Show me what is in my mind and heart that is not pleasing to You. "Examine me, O Lord, and prove me; try my mind and my heart" (Psalm 26:2). Help me to live each day with the love, power, and sound mind You have given me. Give me clarity of thought to replace any confusion.

Being Faithful in Prayer

"Be joyful in hope, patient in affliction, faithful in prayer."

Romans 12:12

Lord, make me to be a person of powerful prayer. Teach me how to be a prayer warrior who is always faithful to pray. I don't want to be someone who prays sporadically, but rather a person so filled with joy and hope that I anticipate great things resulting from each prayer. Help me to have such great faith that I keep praying and never give up.

Put Your
Hope in the Lord

*"May the God of hope fill you with all joy and
peace in believing, that you may abound
in hope by the power of the Holy Spirit."*

ROMANS 15:13 NKJV

LORD, in You I put all my hope and expectations. I
know I have no hope without You (Ephesians 2:12),
so my hope is entirely in You (Psalm 39:7). In the
times I am tempted to feel hopeless—especially
when I don't see answers to my prayers for a long
time and I become discouraged—help me to put
my eyes back on You. Enable me to put a stop to all
feelings of hopelessness in my life. Help me to see
they are not true and that only Your Word is true.

Praying in the Good Times

"Let him who thinks he stands take heed lest he fall."

1 Corinthians 10:12 NKJV

FATHER GOD, I worship You and thank You for Your goodness to me. Thank You for saving me and transforming me for Your high purpose. Help me to remember to pray as fervently to You in the good times as I do in the difficult times. I don't want to ever assume that I can stand strong apart from Your mercy and grace toward me. In my times of blessing I want to pray as fervently as I do in times of struggle.

God Will Make a Way

"No temptation has overtaken you except such as is common to man; but God is faithful, who will not allow you to be tempted beyond what you are able, but with the temptation will also make the way of escape, that you may be able to bear it."

1 Corinthians 10:13 nkjv

Lord, I declare that sin will not have dominion over me, for by Your power and grace I can resist it. I know I can't stand strong if I don't stand on the truth of Your Word. Lord, I thank You that You will not allow me to be tempted beyond what I am able to handle. Thank You for making a way for me to escape temptation (1 Corinthians 10:13). I turn to You, Lord, and ask that by the power of Your Holy Spirit You will help me to withstand any onslaught of the enemy.

TREAT YOUR BODY
AS THOUGH IT
BELONGS TO GOD

*"Whether you eat or drink or whatever
you do, do it all for the glory of God."*

1 CORINTHIANS 10:31

LORD, I commit my body to You as the temple of
Your Holy Spirit. Teach me how to care for it properly. Show me how I should eat and what I should
avoid. Take away all desire for food that is harmful to
me. Give me balance and wisdom. Help me to purify
myself from everything that contaminates my body
and spirit out of reverence for You. Show me where
I allow unnecessary stress to rule in my life, and help
me to take steps to alleviate it. Teach me to simplify
my life, so that I can live better and healthier.

THE IMPORTANCE OF SPIRITUAL AUTHORITY

"For this reason, and because of the angels, the woman ought to have a sign of authority on her head."

1 CORINTHIANS 11:10

LORD, help me to be in right relationship to the authority figures You have put in my life. I know they are there for my protection. I want my life to be in perfect order so I am submitted in the right way. I don't want to do anything that would delay or prevent my becoming all You created me to be. Help me to have a right and submitted heart to You and to them.

HIS WONDERFUL GIFTS

*"Pursue love, and desire spiritual gifts, but
especially that you may prophesy."*

1 CORINTHIANS 14:1 NKJV

❧

THANK YOU, Lord, for Your many gifts to me.
Thank You for Your gifts of salvation, justification,
righteousness, eternal life, and grace. Thank You for
Your gifts of love, peace, and joy. Thank You that
these will never fail in my life because You are my
everlasting Father and You will never fail. Give me
the ability to always have a word in my heart from
You that I can share with others.

Finding
Order and Peace

"For God is not a God of disorder but of peace."

1 Corinthians 14:33

Heavenly Father, I know You are a God of order, and order brings peace. Help me to maintain that same order and peace in my life. Give me the wisdom to not allow anything that would disturb that order and peace to influence my life. Help me to fill my mind with Your Word and my soul with Your Spirit so that there is no room for the enemy's propaganda.

Prayer Grows Love in Your Heart

"And in their prayers for you their hearts will go out to you, because of the surpassing grace God has given you."

2 Corinthians 9:14

LORD, there are certain people I want to pray for because I know You will give me Your heart of love for them. Help me to pray especially for the people who have hurt me. Thank You that praying for others not only changes their lives, but it changes mine as well. I need my heart to be free of hurt, pain, and unforgiveness so that I can love others the way You do.

Stand Strong in Tough Times

"He said to me, 'My grace is sufficient for you, for My strength is made perfect in weakness.' Therefore most gladly I will rather boast in my infirmities, that the power of Christ may rest upon me."

2 Corinthians 12:9 nkjv

Lord, I pray You would help me to stand strong in all I know of You. Teach me to stand on Your Word, no matter what is happening in my life. I acknowledge that I am weak, but I rejoice that You are strong in me—especially during times of trial and difficulty. Help me to learn what I need to know from each challenge I face. Lead me on the path You have for me. I don't want to take a single step without You. Help me in the situation I am facing now. Lift me out of any hopelessness, fear, doubt, or frustration. Enable me to be firm in faith and always abiding in Your will.

When the Failure of Others Tests Our Faith

"Now we pray to God that you will not do anything wrong. Not that people will see that we have stood the test but that you will do what is right even though we may seem to have failed. For we cannot do anything against the truth, but only for the truth. We are glad whenever we are weak but you are strong; and our prayer is for your perfection."

2 Corinthians 13:7-9

Lord God, when I see the failure of any servant of Yours, I pray it will not shake my faith in the least. Help me to do the right thing and remain strong in You no matter what I see anyone else doing. Give me faith that is not dependent on the rise or fall of others. I know You won't fail, even though others do, and that is all that matters.

Trusting in God

*"I have been crucified with Christ; it is no longer I
who live, but Christ lives in me; and the life which
I now live in the flesh I live by faith in the Son of
God, who loved me and gave Himself for me."*

GALATIANS 2:20 NKJV

LORD, You are everything to me. I know that
because of You I am never without love, joy, hope,
power, protection, and provision. Because of You
I can rise above my limitations and live in peace,
knowing You will work things out for my good
as I live Your way. Open my eyes more and more
to Your truth. Enable me to recognize and understand Your promises to me so that I can successfully choose to reject all doubt in my life. Help me
to trust You in all things every day.

Moving into the Freedom God Has for Us

*"It is for freedom that Christ has set us free.
Stand firm, then, and do not let yourselves
be burdened again by a yoke of slavery."*

Galatians 5:1

LORD, help me to stand firm in the freedom You have secured for me. Thank You, Jesus, that You gave Your life so that I could be set free from the yoke of slavery to the enemy of my soul. Help me to not become entangled in it again. Make me aware when I am accepting some bondage in my life for which You died to set me free.

Live in Healthy Relationships

"Through love serve one another. For all the law is fulfilled in one word, even in this: 'You shall love your neighbor as yourself.'"

Galatians 5:13-14 nkjv

Lord, I pray You would send people into my life who are godly, wise, and strong in their knowledge of You. Help us to contribute to the quality of each other's lives. Help me to always exhibit Your love to others. Help me to love others as myself (Galatians 5:14). Help me to always be quick to forgive in any relationship. Show me the relationships that are worth fighting for, and help me to see when a relationship will always be destructive no matter what I do. Enable me to move with the leading of Your Holy Spirit in this. I ask You to be in charge of all of my relationships so that they will be what You want them to be.

Bow Down
Before His Holiness

*"He chose us in Him before the foundation
of the world, that we should be holy and
without blame before Him in love."*

EPHESIANS 1:4 NKJV

LORD, You are mighty and have done great things
for me. Holy is Your name. Help me to continually maintain a humble heart of worship before You.
You are worthy of all praise and honor and glory, for
only You are holy. "O LORD, You are my God. I will
exalt You, I will praise Your name, for You have done
wonderful things" (Isaiah 25:1). I sing praise to You,
LORD, and give thanks at the remembrance of Your
holy name (Psalm 30:4). I bow and worship You in
the beauty of Your holiness (Psalm 29:2).

Seeing the Power of God at Work

"I pray also that the eyes of your heart may be enlightened in order that you may know the hope to which he has called you, the riches of his glorious inheritance in the saints, and his incomparably great power for us who believe."

Ephesians 1:18-19

Dear God, I pray the eyes of my heart will be opened to see the hope to which You have called me. Help me to understand my true glorious inheritance. Enable me to comprehend the magnitude of Your power on my behalf because I believe in You. I seek more of Your presence and Your power so that I can see them manifested in my life.

LIVING IN HIS GRACE

"To each one of us grace was given according to the measure of Christ's gift."

EPHESIANS 4:7 NKJV

LORD, Your unfailing love is a great comfort to me. Thank You that nothing can separate me from Your love (Romans 8:35). Thank You for Your grace that gives me far better than I deserve. Thank You, Jesus, for taking the consequences of my sin. I pray You will teach me all the "mysteries of the kingdom of heaven" (Matthew 13:11). Help me to seek Your kingdom every day and to live in the gifts You have given me.

MOVE IN FORGIVENESS—
GOD'S AND YOURS

*"Be kind to one another, tenderhearted, forgiving
one another, even as God in Christ forgave you."*

EPHESIANS 4:32 NKJV

LORD, I thank You for forgiving me and not even remembering my sins anymore (Hebrews 8:12). Show me anything I need to confess to You today so that I can bring it before You and be set free. I especially ask that You would reveal any place in my heart where I have not forgiven someone. I don't want to live in unforgiveness anymore, for any reason. Help me to be a forgiving person in the same way You are forgiving toward me. Help me to always forgive quickly and not wait for the other person to say or do what I think they should.

Getting Armed
for the Battle

*"Put on the full armor of God so that you can take
your stand against the devil's schemes…Pray
in the Spirit on all occasions with all kinds of
prayers and requests. With this in mind, be alert
and always keep on praying for all the saints."*

EPHESIANS 6:11,18

LORD, because I have aligned myself with You, the
enemy wages war against me. Help me to put on the
full spiritual armor You have provided for me. Teach
me what that is so I understand how to maintain
it. Help me to fully understand the depth of truth,
righteousness, faith, a solid walk with Christ, salvation, powerful prayer, and the sword of the Spirit,
which is Your Word. Help me to live in that.

PRAYER AND THANKSGIVING BRING PEACE

*"Do not be anxious about anything, but in
everything, by prayer and petition, with
thanksgiving, present your requests to God.
And the peace of God, which transcends
all understanding, will guard your hearts
and your minds in Christ Jesus."*

PHILIPPIANS 4:6-7

DEAR GOD, help me to not be anxious or worried about anything. Help me to pray and intercede instead. Enable me to lift up praise and worship in the face of whatever opposes me. Help me to bring every concern before You and leave it at Your feet. Help me to refuse to think what-if thoughts. Fill me with Your peace that passes all understanding so that my heart and mind will be protected.

The Power of
Praying for Others

"For this reason, since the day we heard about you, we have not stopped praying for you and asking God to fill you with the knowledge of his will through all spiritual wisdom and understanding."

COLOSSIANS 1:9

LORD, I pray for the people You have put in my life and on my heart. Fill them with wisdom and understanding and the knowledge of Your will so that they will stay on the path You have for them. I pray they will learn to hear Your voice and come to know You better, so that they can have a closer walk with You. I pray that for myself as well.

Waiting for Answers

*"Continue earnestly in prayer, being
vigilant in it with thanksgiving."*

Colossians 4:2 nkjv

Lord, I know Your judgments are perfect, and so I will praise You above all things—even my own desires and expectations. Nothing will shake me, not even seemingly unanswered prayers. When I can't see the answers to my prayers, open my eyes to see things from Your perspective. I am grateful that You, who are the all-powerful, all-knowing God of the universe, are also my heavenly Father, who loves me unconditionally and will never forsake me. Thank You for hearing and answering my prayers.

How to Always Do God's Will

"Be joyful always; pray continually; give thanks in all circumstances, for this is God's will for you in Christ Jesus."

1 Thessalonians 5:16-18

God, I know it is always Your will for me to be joyful and pray often and give thanks to You in all circumstances. Help me to remember to do Your will in this regard, even when I don't see answers to my prayers as I would like. No matter what is happening in my life, I know You are greater than anything I face. Even in difficult times, I want to do Your will in every way.

PRAYING FOR PEOPLE
WHO NEED GOOD NEWS

*"Finally, brothers, pray for us that the
message of the Lord may spread rapidly and
be honored, just as it was with you."*

2 THESSALONIANS 3:1

LORD, use me to bring the good news of salvation through Jesus Christ to others. Just as You have used others powerfully in my life, equip me with the right words at the right time so that those whose hearts are ready will be drawn toward You. I also pray for the men and women who need the good news, that their hearts would be open to receive all You have for them.

PRAYING TOGETHER
IN UNITY

*"I want men everywhere to lift up holy hands
in prayer, without anger or disputing."*

1 TIMOTHY 2:8

LORD, help me to find other believers who will stand with me in prayer. Bring godly prayer partners into my life with whom I can pray in power. Help us to be so devoted to You that we maintain a oneness of the Spirit, even if we disagree on certain things. I pray we will be unified in our belief in Your Word so that we will be unified in our prayers.

REMEMBERING
OTHERS IN PRAYER

*"I thank God, whom I serve, as my forefathers
did, with a clear conscience, as night and day
I constantly remember you in my prayers."*

2 TIMOTHY 1:3

LORD, help me to not forget anyone in my prayers.
Especially show me the people who feel forgotten so
that I can remember them in intercession. Bring specific people to mind who need a miracle of healing or
help. Show me who needs to hear Your voice guiding
them. Enable the people I pray for to sense Your love
in their lives. Show me what more I can do.

ASK FOR BOLDNESS TO SHARE YOUR FAITH

"I pray that you may be active in sharing your faith, so that you will have a full understanding of every good thing we have in Christ."

PHILEMON 1:6

GOD, help me to get over any inhibitions I have about sharing my faith with unbelievers. I know of no greater gift than to give someone Your love and the good news of salvation in Christ, but I always want to be sensitive to Your leading so that I don't come off as insensitive to others. Help me to always have a perfect sense of timing and the right words to say.

Take God at His Word

"The word of God is living and powerful, and sharper than any two-edged sword, piercing even to the division of soul and spirit, and of joints and marrow, and is a discerner of the thoughts and intents of the heart."

Hebrews 4:12 nkjv

Lord, help me to meditate on Your Word every day and night so that I can be like a tree planted by a river that brings forth fruit and doesn't wither, so that whatever I do will prosper (Psalm 1:1-3). Enable me to live Your way so that my prayers are always pleasing in Your sight (Proverbs 28:9). Your Word reveals what is in my heart. I pray You will cleanse my heart of all evil and expose anything that is not Your will for my life. Teach me the right way to live so that my life will work the way You intend for it to do.

APPROACH GOD'S THRONE
WITH CONFIDENCE

*"For we do not have a high priest who is unable
to sympathize with our weaknesses, but we
have one who has been tempted in every
way, just as we are—yet was without sin. Let
us then approach the throne of grace with
confidence, so that we may receive mercy and
find grace to help us in our time of need."*

HEBREWS 4:15-16

THANK YOU, Jesus, that You understand my weaknesses and my temptations, for You have been tempted in every way and yet did not sin. Because You understand my struggles, I know I can come to You and receive help. Enable me to approach You with confidence, knowing You will sustain me in my time of need.

Replace Doubt with Unwavering Faith

*"Without faith it is impossible to please
Him, for he who comes to God must believe
that He is, and that He is a rewarder
of those who diligently seek Him."*

Hebrews 11:6 NKJV

Jesus, thank You for the gift of faith You have given me. Increase my faith every day as I read Your Word. Give me strong faith to believe for the answers to my prayers. I know it is not about me trying to establish great faith on my own. That comes from Your Spirit and Your Word. I know that "whatever is not from faith is sin," so I confess all doubt within me (Romans 14:23). I pray You will make me to be so strong in faith that I will always be pleasing to You.

HEARING GOD'S VOICE

*"May the God of peace…make you complete in
every good work to do His will, working in you
what is well pleasing in His sight, through Jesus
Christ, to whom be glory forever and ever."*

HEBREWS 13:20-21 NKJV

LORD, help me to refuse to hold on to things that
are not of You. Help me to cling to You instead of
my own dreams. When I experience difficult times,
help me to know if it is because I have done something wrong, or if it is that I have done something
right and this is happening according to Your will.
Lord, only You know what is right for me. Help me
to hear Your voice leading me. Transform me to do
Your will. Help me to have endurance so that I can
receive the promises of all You have for me.

GOING THROUGH TRIALS WITH GOD'S STRENGTH

"My brethren, count it all joy when you fall into various trials, knowing that the testing of your faith produces patience. But let patience have its perfect work, that you may be perfect and complete, lacking nothing."

JAMES 1:2-4 NKJV

LORD, thank You for helping me stand strong. You have armed me with strength for the battle. Help me to become so strong in You that I can stand without wavering, no matter what happens. Teach me to rest in You, knowing that You will give me what I need for the moment I am in. I am determined to "count it all joy" when I go through trials, because of the perfecting work You will do for me (James 1:2-4). "Though I walk in the midst of trouble, You will revive me" (Psalm 138:7).

Asking God for Wisdom

"If any of you lacks wisdom, he should ask God, who gives generously to all without finding fault, and it will be given to him."

James 1:5

God, I ask for wisdom, for I know true wisdom comes only from You. Thank You that Your Word promises You will give wisdom to me when I ask for it. Help me to be wise every day in every decision, especially when I must act quickly. Help me to know what to do and what not to do in any situation. Thank You for Your generosity to me.

Learning to Believe

*"Let him ask in faith, with no doubting,
for he who doubts is like a wave of the
sea driven and tossed by the wind."*

James 1:6

DEAR GOD, increase my faith to believe for great things. Help me to have faith enough to not pray too small. I know it is not about trusting in faith itself, but trusting in You. It's not about believing in my own ability to believe, but rather it is believing in Your ability and promise to hear and answer. Take away all unbelief in me.

Powerful and Effective Praying

"Therefore confess your sins to each other and pray for each other so that you may be healed. The prayer of a righteous man is powerful and effective."

James 5:16

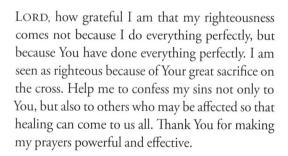

Lord, how grateful I am that my righteousness comes not because I do everything perfectly, but because You have done everything perfectly. I am seen as righteous because of Your great sacrifice on the cross. Help me to confess my sins not only to You, but also to others who may be affected so that healing can come to us all. Thank You for making my prayers powerful and effective.

GOD HEARS OUR PRAYERS
AND SEES OUR HEART

*"For the eyes of the Lord are on the righteous and
his ears are attentive to their prayer, but the
face of the Lord is against those who do evil."*

1 PETER 3:12

DEAR GOD, I thank You that You see my heart
and hear my prayers. How grateful I am that when
You see me, You see the righteousness of Jesus *in*
me and not the sinner I was before I received Him
into my life. Thank You that You not only hear my
prayers, but You see my need and will answer the
cries of my heart.

Say "No Way" to Temptation

"Be sober, be vigilant; because your adversary the devil walks about like a roaring lion, seeking whom he may devour. Resist him, steadfast in the faith, knowing that the same sufferings are experienced by your brotherhood in the world."

1 Peter 5:8-9 nkjv

Lord, I pray You would lead me far away from all temptation to do or think anything that is not pleasing to You. Help me to always know what is right and enable me to do it. Deliver me from all attacks of the evil one, who tries to entice me away from what is good in Your sight. I pray that the weakness of my flesh will be overcome by the strength and power of Your Spirit. I know that I am dead to sin but alive in Christ Jesus, and therefore I will not allow sin to reign in me.

FINDING FORGIVENESS
THROUGH CONFESSION

"If we confess our sins, he is faithful and just and will forgive us our sins and purify us from all unrighteousness."

1 JOHN 1:9

LORD, I confess my sins before You. Thank You that You are faithful to forgive them and to cleanse me from all the effects of them. If there is sin in my life that I am not seeing, reveal it to me now so that I can confess it before You and be purified of all unrighteousness. I want a repentant heart, because I want to live in the wholeness of complete forgiveness.

WELCOME GOD'S WILL AND DO IT

"The world is passing away, and the lust of it; but
he who does the will of God abides forever."

1 JOHN 2:17 NKJV

LORD, I pray You would teach me to do Your will.
Work the desire for Your will into my heart. I am
grateful to You that Your will can be known. Guide
my every step so that I don't make a wrong decision
or take a wrong path. Fill me with the knowledge
of Your will in all wisdom and spiritual understanding (Colossians 1:9). Line the desires of my heart
up with the desires of Your heart. I want what You
want for my life.

BASK IN GOD'S LOVE

"Beloved, let us love one another, for love is of God; and everyone who loves is born of God and knows God. He who does not love does not know God, for God is love."

1 JOHN 4:7-8 NKJV

LORD, I thank You that You are the God of love. Thank You for loving me even before I knew You. Thank You for sending Your Son, Jesus, to die for me and take on Himself all I deserve. Thank You, Jesus, that You have given me life with You forever, and a better life now. Your love heals me and makes me whole. "You are my Lord, my goodness is nothing apart from You" (Psalm 16:2). I know there is a great dimension of healing and wholeness that can only happen in the presence of Your love. Enable me to open up to Your love working in my life like never before. Wash over me with Your love today.

Receive All Jesus Died for You to Have

"We have seen and testify that the Father has sent the Son as Savior of the world. Whoever confesses that Jesus is the Son of God, God abides in him, and he in God."

1 John 4:14-15 NKJV

Lord Jesus, I know You came "to seek and to save that which was lost" (Luke 19:10). Thank You that You saw my lost condition and have saved me for Yourself and Your purposes. Thank You that because You died for me, I have eternal life and Your blood cleanses me from all sin (1 John 1:7). Now I can live free of guilt and condemnation. I believe "there is no other name under heaven" by which I could ever be saved (Acts 4:12).

Coming to Father God in Confidence

"This is the confidence we have in approaching God: that if we ask anything according to his will, he hears us. And if we know that he hears us—whatever we ask—we know that we have what we asked of him."

1 John 5:14-15

Heavenly Father, it gives me great confidence to know that if I ask according to Your will, You will hear me and I will have what I ask for. I come to You as Your beloved child and ask You to help me pray according to Your will. I know I will receive only good things from You because You love and accept me.

Prayer Rises

*"The smoke of the incense, together
with the prayers of the saints, went up
before God from the angel's hand."*

Revelation 8:4

Lord, how grateful I am that my prayers always
rise to You in heaven and You hear each one. Even
the quietest prayers of my heart born out of faith
are as important as my loudest prayers ignited by
fervency. Thank You that You will hear and answer
them all. How blessed am I to have You as the cen-
ter of my life.

Praising God for the Future

"Let us rejoice and be glad and give him glory! For the wedding of the Lamb has come, and his bride has made herself ready."

Revelation 19:7

Lord God, I praise You for my future, for You have promised that it is good. Thank You that my ultimate end is with You in heaven. I praise You for Your future redemption of the world and of all things in my life. As I worship You now, I thank You that one day I will worship You face-to-face for all eternity. I look hopefully forward to that day.

Other Books
by Stormie Omartian

The Power of a Praying® Life
In this book Stormie helps readers find the freedom, wholeness, and true success God has for them. She gives them practical ways to make their life work.

The Power of Praying® for Your Adult Children
For more than 15 years, millions of parents have prayed for their children using Stormie's book *The Power of a Praying® Parent*. As children become adults, they need prayer just as much, and Stormie has provided new, helpful, and effective ways for every parent to pray and find peace in the process.

The Power of Prayer™ to Change Your Marriage
Stormie gives 14 ways to meet the 14 challenges to every marriage so that your marriage can last a lifetime. This is the follow-up book to her bestselling books *The Power of a Praying® Wife* and *The Power of a Praying® Husband*.

Just Enough Light for the Step I'm On
All Christians, especially those experiencing life changes or difficult times, will appreciate Stormie's honesty, candor, and advice, based on experience and the Word of God, as she show readers how to walk in peace through the pressures of today's world.

The Power of a Praying® Woman
Stormie Omartian's bestselling books have helped hundreds of thousands of individuals pray more effectively for their spouses, their children, and their nation. Now she has written a book on a subject she knows intimately: being a praying woman. Stormie's deep knowledge of Scripture and candid examples from her own prayer life provide guidance for women who seek to trust God with deep longings and cover every area of life with prayer.